Alice Richardson is a barrister at Trinity Chambers, based in Newcastle upon Tyne, where she is Deputy Head of the Civil Team. She was called to the Bar in 2013 and has specialised in property, housing, local government and public law throughout her career.

Alice frequently advises and represents clients at all stages of housing licensing from designation through to enforcement including prosecutions, appeals and judicial review. Her experience informs the practical focus of this book.

A Practitioner's Guide to Housing Licensing and Enforcement

A Practitioner's Guide to Housing Licensing and Enforcement

Alice Richardson

Barrister

Trinity Chambers

Law Brief Publishing

Published 2026 by Law Brief Publishing, an imprint of Law Brief Publishing Ltd
30 The Parks
Minehead
Somerset
TA24 8BT

www.lawbriefpublishing.com

Paperback: 978-1-918241-33-4

For my boys, Finn and Oisin, who were disappointed to learn I am not, in fact, Batman.

PREFACE

Housing licensing sits at the intersection of multiple disciplines: criminal and regulatory law, housing and property law, and public law and local government.

There remains limited practitioner literature addressing licensing in a fully integrated way. Licensing enforcement may therefore appear specialist or complex, even though it increasingly forms part of everyday advisory and litigation work.

This book is intended to provide a structured and practical account of that framework.

It is written for lawyers and advisers who may not consider themselves housing specialists but are asked to advise on licensing, enforcement or the consequences of non-compliance. It is equally directed at local authority lawyers and officers making regulatory decisions, and at those representing landlords or agents facing criminal or civil enforcement.

The importance of this area continues to grow. In England the Renters' Rights Act 2025 places renewed emphasis on effective enforcement. In Wales, the Housing (Wales) Act 2014 operates alongside the Housing Act 2004 and created a distinct but related regulatory structure. As enforcement powers expand, so too does the need for lawyers who are comfortable operating across regulatory, criminal, tribunal and public law forums.

For practitioners, this presents both challenge and opportunity. Licensing enforcement is no longer niche. It is a developing area in which lawyers with a clear understanding of the statutory framework and procedural routes can add real value—whether advising authorities, landlords, agents or tenants.

In that sense, this book aims to reassure as much as to inform. Housing licensing enforcement applies familiar legal principles within a defined statutory context. With a structured approach, these cases are manageable and intellectually rewarding.

The hope is that this book equips practitioners with the confidence to engage with this work directly: to advise clearly, to challenge decisions where appropriate, and to take or defend enforcement action lawfully and effectively.

The law stated in this book is believed to be accurate and up to date as at 1st January 2026.

I would like to thank everyone at Trinity Chambers and beyond who has supported me since I returned to self-employed practice. The last few years have not always been easy but coming home to Newcastle and to Chambers has meant everything.

Thank you to Garry Wright and Tim Kevan for the additional challenge of writing my first book, and for their patience throughout the process.

Finally, thank you to my mum, for all the babysitting. And to Callum, for keeping me sane(ish).

Alice Richardson
March 2026

CONTENTS

PART I	THE STATUTORY LICENSING FRAMEWORK	1
Chapter One	Introduction and Legislative Context	3
Chapter Two	What Is a House in Multiple Occupation?	7
Chapter Three	Mandatory Licensing	17
Chapter Four	Additional Licensing	23
Chapter Five	Selective Licensing Under Part 3	27
Chapter Six	Landlord Registration and Licensing in Wales	35
PART II	LICENSING PROCEDURE AND LIABILITY	41
Chapter Seven	Applications, Grant, Variation, Revocation and Appeals	43
Chapter Eight	Who Is Responsible?	49
Chapter Nine	Licence Conditions	53

PART III	CRIMINAL AND CIVIL ENFORCEMENT	61
Chapter Ten	Criminal Offences and Prosecution	63
Chapter Eleven	Civil Penalties	69
Chapter Twelve	Rent Repayment Orders	75
Chapter Thirteen	Banning Orders, Management Orders & the Rogue Landlord Database	85
Chapter Fourteen	Investigatory Powers	91
PART IV	HOUSING LICENSING IN PRACTICE	95
Chapter Fifteen	Practical Compliance and Enforcement Strategy	97

PART I

THE STATUTORY LICENSING FRAMEWORK

CHAPTER ONE

INTRODUCTION AND LEGISLATIVE CONTEXT

The modern system of housing licensing must be understood against the growth and changing role of the private rented sector. According to the English Housing Survey 2024–25, the private rented sector in England accounts for approximately 4.7 million households, representing around 19% of all households. Throughout the 1980s and 1990s, the proportion of households renting privately remained relatively stable, at between 9% and 11%. The sector expanded rapidly during the early 2000s, effectively doubling in size, but has since stabilised at approximately 19–20% of households since 2013–14.

This expansion altered the character of the housing market. Private renting is no longer a marginal tenure. It accommodates families, long-term occupiers, students, migrant workers and vulnerable households. That growth, and the increasingly diverse population reliant upon the sector, formed the legislative backdrop to the Housing Act 2004.

The Housing Act 2004 Framework

Parts 2 and 3 of the Housing Act 2004 came into force in April 2006. For the first time, a structured statutory licensing regime was introduced across England and Wales, directed at improving standards in the private rented sector and addressing ineffective management.

The Act established three principal licensing regimes:

- Mandatory licensing, applying to prescribed categories of houses in multiple occupation (HMOs);
- Additional licensing, enabling local housing authorities to extend licensing to further HMOs within designated areas;
- Selective licensing, permitting the licensing of other privately rented housing within designated areas where statutory conditions are satisfied.

Licensing was not conceived as a standalone administrative requirement. It formed part of a broader regulatory architecture, operating alongside the hazard-based enforcement system under Part 1 of the Act and supported by criminal sanctions and management interventions.

Each regime requires the grant of a licence, the imposition of mandatory and discretionary conditions, and the identification of a licence holder and manager who must be fit and proper persons. From its inception, the scheme linked regulatory compliance to enforceable legal consequences.

Failure to obtain a required licence or to comply with licence conditions may result in:

- criminal prosecution;
- civil financial penalties;
- rent repayment orders;
- banning orders;
- restrictions on possession proceedings.

Where England and Wales diverge

Parts 2 and 3 of the Housing Act 2004 apply in both England and Wales. The core statutory definitions of HMOs (sections 254–259), the designation powers (sections 56–60 and sections 80–84), and the offence provisions remain common to both jurisdictions.

However, subsequent legislative developments have diverged.

In England, the scope of mandatory HMO licensing was expanded in October 2018 through secondary legislation removing the three-storey requirement and introducing national minimum room sizes.

The 2018 reforms removed the storey requirement and extended mandatory licensing to all HMOs occupied by five or more persons forming two or more households, regardless of height. National minimum sleeping room sizes were introduced and waste disposal requirements strengthened.

The practical effect was a significant increase in the number of licensable properties and, correspondingly, an expansion of enforcement activity.

In Wales, two major pieces of devolved legislation reshape the context in which licensing operates. First, the Housing (Wales) Act 2014 introduced a separate landlord registration and licensing scheme (Rent Smart Wales), requiring landlords and letting agents to be registered and, in certain cases, licensed in order to carry out letting and management activities.

Secondly, the Renting Homes (Wales) Act 2016, fully implemented in December 2022, replaced traditional tenancy categories with a system of "occupation contracts". The 2016 Act alters the contractual and possession framework within which private renting operates in Wales. While it does not displace the Housing Act 2004 licensing regimes, it affects enforcement consequences, possession restrictions, and the practical operation of landlord compliance.

By contrast, in England, reform has proceeded primarily through amendments to the Housing Act 2004, the Housing and Planning Act 2016, and most recently the Renters' Rights Act 2025.

The statutory core of licensing therefore remains shared, but the wider tenancy and regulatory environment now differs materially between England and Wales. Where those differences affect licensing and enforcement practice, they are identified in the chapters that follow.

CHAPTER TWO

WHAT IS A HOUSE IN MULTIPLE OCCUPATION?

Part 2 of the Housing Act 2004 provides for a scheme for local authorities to require the licencing of houses in multiple occupation (HMOs). Subject to exceptions, every HMO to which Pt 2 applies must be licensed: section 61(1).

Before considering whether a property is an HMO which is required to be licensed it is necessary to consider whether the property is an HMO at all.

Disputes as to whether or not the definition is satisfied are common and frequently form the basis of challenges to enforcement action. The statutory scheme requires careful attention to the relevant definitions and tests.

Statutory Framework

Section 77 provides, for the purposes of Part 2, that "HMO" means a house in multiple occupation as defined by sections 254 to 259 and includes any yard, garden, outhouses and appurtenances belonging to or usually enjoyed with it. By section 254(1) a building, or part of a building, is an HMO if :

(a) it satisfies 'the standard test' (section 254(2));

(b) it satisfies 'the self-contained flat test' (section 254(3));

(c) it satisfies the 'converted building test' (section 254(4));

(d) an HMO declaration is in force in respect of it under section 255; or

(e) it is a converted block of flats to which section 257 applies.

Each test must be considered separately. A property may fall within more than one category, but need only satisfy one to constitute an HMO for the purposes of the Act.

The Standard HMO Test

Under section 254(2), a building or part of a building meets the standard test if–

(a) it consists of one or more units of living accommodation not consisting of a self-contained flat or flats;

(b) the living accommodation is occupied by persons who do not form a single household;

(c) the living accommodation is occupied by those persons as their only or main residence or they are to be treated as so occupying it;

(d) their occupation of the living accommodation constitutes the only use of that accommodation;

(e) rents are payable or other consideration is to be provided in respect of at least one of those persons' occupation of the living accommodation; and

(f) two or more of the households who occupy the living accommodation share one or more basic amenities or the living accommodation is lacking in one or more basic amenities.

This is the most commonly applied test and captures the typical shared house or bedsit accommodation. Each element of the test must be satisfied.

Particular issues often arise in relation to the identification of separate households and whether occupation is as an only or main residence.

'Occupied by persons who do not form a single household'

Under section 262(6) an "occupier" is a person who occupies residential premises whether as a tenant, or a person with an estate or interest in the premises, or a licensee. It is not therefore necessary for the occupiers to be tenants.

Section 258 sets out when persons are to be regarded as not forming a single household for the purposes of section 254. Persons are to be regarded as not forming a single household unless (a) they are members of the same family or (b) their circumstances are specified in regulations: section 258(2).

A person is a member of the same family as another person if (a) they are a couple (married, civil partners or live together as if they were) (b) one of them is a relative of the other; or (c) one of them is, or is a relative of, one member of a couple and the other is a relative of the other member of the couple: section 258(3)

"Relative" means parent, grandparent, child, grandchild, brother, sister, uncle, aunt, nephew, niece or cousin. A stepchild is treated as a child and "a relationship of the half-blood shall be treated as a relationship of the whole blood": section 258(4).

A foster child will be regarded as part of a single household with his or her foster parent if placed there under the provisions of the Fostering Services Regulations 2002 (SI 2002/57).

Persons carrying out work of a 'domestic nature' (such as au pairs, nannies, maids and personal assistances) are considered part of a single household where live-in accommodation is provided as part of the payment for work. As are members of that persons family who live with them: The Licensing and Management of Houses in Multiple Occupation and Other Houses (Miscellaneous Provisions) (England) Regulations 2006 (SI 2006/373), The Licensing and Management of Houses in Multiple Occupation and Other Houses (Miscellaneous Provisions) (Wales) Regulations 2006 (SI 2006/1715).

There are also provisions for a person receiving care from an approved placement carer and his or her carer who occupy the same building or part of a building under the Adult Placement Schemes (England) Regulations 2004 (SI 2004/2071) and Adult Placement Schemes (Wales) Regulations 2004 (SI 2004/1756).

'Only or Main Residence'

Whether a person occupies property as their only or main residence is a question of fact. Guidance on the quality of occupation which is required and factors which will indicate that the requirement is satisfied can be taken from case law and the question arises in various different statutory contexts, but it remains question of fact in each case (see *Opara v Olasemo* [2020] UKUT 96 (LC) and *Camfield v Uyiekpen* [2022] UKUT 234 (LC); [2022] HLR 48).

Certain occupiers, however, are deemed to be occupying the property as their only or main residence even though their principal home may be elsewhere including full-time students, occupiers of refuges, migrant workers accommodated by their employers and asylum seekers being accommodated by the National Asylum Support Service: section 259 and reg.5, Licensing and Management of Houses in Multiple Occupation and Other Houses (Miscellaneous Provisions) (England) Regulations 2006 (SI 2006/373), and reg.5, Licensing and Management of Houses in Multiple Occupation and Other Houses (Miscellaneous Provisions) (Wales) Regulations 2006 (SI 2006/1715).

Occupation of the living accommodation must constitute the occupiers' only or main residence. Section 260 of the Housing Act 2004 creates a rebuttable presumption that this requirement is satisfied.

In practice, difficulty may arise where the nature of occupation fluctuates, making it unclear whether the accommodation is being used as the residents' only or main residence at any given time. This issue commonly arises in premises such as hotels or hostels which may, at different times, accommodate short-term visitors and longer-term residents who have no other home. In such cases, the assessment turns on the factual use of the accommodation rather than its formal designation or intended purpose.

The sole use condition.

The occupation of the living accommodation must constitute the only use of that accommodation (section 254(2)(d)). Section 260 creates a rebuttable presumption in any proceedings that this condition is met, placing the burden on the party asserting that other concurrent uses exist.

The meaning of section 254(2)(d) was authoritatively determined by the Court of Appeal in *Global 100 Ltd v Jimenez* [2023] EWCA Civ 1243; [2024] 1 WLR 1775. The case concerned property guardians; individuals licensed by a guardian company to occupy empty commercial buildings in return for a weekly fee, on the basis that their presence deterred trespass and vandalism. The guardian company argued that the guardians' occupation served two purposes (residence and security) and therefore did not constitute the only use of the living accommodation.

The Court of Appeal dismissed the appeals and held that s.254(2)(d) focuses on the use the occupiers make of their living accommodation, not the purpose of the guardian company in placing them there. Use and purpose are conceptually distinct: the guardians' use was to live in the accommodation as their main residence; the company's purpose in facilitating that occupation was the protection of its client's building. The incidental deterrent effect of the guardians' presence did not introduce a second use of the living accommodation. As Dingemans LJ put it at para 50, the provision concerns the use made by the property guardians of their living accommodation, their occupation of it, 77and not the guardian company's purpose in allowing them to reside there. The Court reached this conclusion on the facts without needing to rely on the s.260 presumption.

Sharing basic amenities

Two or more of the households which occupy the living accommodation must share one or more of the basic amenities or the living accommodation must be lacking in one or more of those facilities.

Basic amenities are defined at section 254(8) as meaning (a) a toilet (b) personal washing facilities or (c) cooking facilities.

The Self-Contained Flat Test

By Section 254(3) a part of a building meets the self- contained flat test if it is a self-contained flat and paragraphs (b)-(f) of section 254(2) apply (reading references to the living accommodation as references to the flat).

It is essentially the same as the standard test but applies to a self-contained flat. Self-contained flat is defined at section 254(8) as a separate set of premises (whether or not on the same floor) (a) which forms part of a building (b) either the whole or a material part of which lies above or below some other part of the building and (c) all three basic amenities are available for the exclusive use of its occupants.

This test therefore covers shared flats, including those let on a room-by-room basis with shared basic amenities.

The Converted Building Test

By Section 254(4) a building or a part of a building meets the converted building test if-

(a) it is a converted building (defined in section 254(8) as a building or part of a building consisting of living accommodation in which one or more units of such accommodation have been created since the building or part was constructed);

(b) it contains one or more units of living accommodation that do not consist of a self-contained flat or flats (whether or not it also contains any such flat or flats);

(c) the living accommodation is occupied by persons who do not form a single household (see section 258);

(d) the living accommodation is occupied by those persons as their only or main residence or they are to be treated as so occupying it (see section 259);

(e) their occupation of the living accommodation constitutes the only use of that accommodation; and

(f) rents are payable or other consideration is to be provided in respect of at least one of those persons' occupation of the living accommodation.

HMO Declarations

Section 255 enables a local housing authority to make a HMO declaration where occupation of the living accommodation amounts to a "significant use" of the property (rather than sole use) and the other elements of either the standard test, self-contained flat test or converted building test are satisfied. The Act does not define "significant use" but it is commonly used where mixed-use accommodation has a fluctuating pattern of occupation such that it is unclear whether the sole use requirement is satisfied at any given time.

To make an HMO declaration a local housing authority must serve a notice which must (a) state the date of the authority's decision to serve the notice; (b) be served on each relevant person within the period of seven days beginning with the date of that decision; (c) state the day on which it will come into force if no appeal is made, which must be not less than 28 days after the date of the authority's decision (s.255(5)); and (d) set out the right to appeal against the decision and the period within which an appeal may be made.

By section 255(12) a relevant person is defined as any person who, to the authority's knowledge, has an estate or interest in the building or part of the building concerned (other than a tenant under a lease with an unexpired term of three years or less); or is a person managing or having control of the building, within the meaning of section 263 (see Chapter 8).

Where no appeal is made, the declaration takes effect on the date specified in the notice: section 255(6).

A relevant person may appeal against an HMO declaration to the First-tier Tribunal (in England) or the residential property tribunal (in Wales) within 28 days beginning with the date of the authority's decision: section 255(9). Where an appeal is made in time, the declaration does not come into force unless and until it is confirmed by the tribunal and the time for appealing to the Upper Tribunal has expired, or any further appeal is withdrawn or determined: section 255(7)-(8).

An appeal is by way of rehearing, but the tribunal may take into account matters of which the authority was unaware at the time of its decision: section 255(10) (see Chapter 7).

Section 257 HMOs

Section 257 creates a distinct category of HMO relating to certain converted blocks of flats. Where a building or part of a building which (a) has been converted into, and (b) consists of, self-contained flats the section applies if-

(a) building work undertaken in connection with the conversion did not comply with the appropriate building standards (defined in section 257(3)) and still does not comply with them; and

(b) less than two-thirds of the self-contained flats are owner-occupied (defined in section 257(4)).

The fact that this section applies to a converted block of flats (with the result that it is HMO under section 254(1)(e)) does not affect the status of any individual flat in the block as a house in multiple occupation.

CHAPTER THREE

MANDATORY LICENSING

Part 2 of the Housing Act 2004 establishes a system of licensing for certain HMOs.

First, it must be determined whether a building or part of a building constitutes an HMO (addressed in Chapter 2).

Next, it must be determined whether that HMO falls within Part 2. Section 55(2) identifies two categories of HMOs to which Part 2 may apply:

- HMOs of a prescribed description, which are subject to mandatory licensing (section 55(2)(a)); and
- HMOs of a description specified in a designation made by a local housing authority under section 56 (additional licensing).

This chapter is concerned with the mandatory licensing scheme and additional licensing is dealt with in Chapter 4, though many of same principles apply.

HMOs subject to Mandatory Licensing

From 1 October 2018, in England, a HMO is of a prescribed description if it is occupied by five or more persons living in two or more separate households and it meets the standard test, the self-contained flat test (but is not a purpose-built flat situated in a block comprising three or more self-contained flats) or the converted building test: Licensing of Houses in Multiple Occupation (Prescribed Description) (England) Order (SI 2018/221).

Prior to October 2018, the prescribed description for mandatory HMO licensing was narrower and applied only to HMOs which were occupied by five or more persons forming two or more households and consisted of three or more storeys.

Although the storey requirement has been removed in England, it continues to apply in Wales: Licensing of Houses in Multiple Occupation (Prescribed Descriptions) (Wales) Order 2006 (SI 2006/1712).

Exemptions

Section 254(5) provides that a HMO which would fall within section 254(1) is not a HMO for the purposes of the Act (other than Part 1) if it is listed in Schedule 14. The principal exclusions are as follows:

- Buildings managed or controlled by public bodies such as local housing authorities and registered social landlords (Sch. 14, paras 1–2).
- Buildings subject to alternative statutory regulatory regimes (Sch. 14, para. 3).
- Purpose-built or managed student accommodation meeting the statutory criteria (Sch. 14, para. 4).
- Buildings occupied by religious communities (Sch. 14, para. 5).

- Buildings occupied by owner-occupiers, members of their household and no more than two other persons (Sch. 14, para. 6 and reg.6(2) of the Licensing and Management of Houses in Multiple Occupation and Other Houses (Miscellaneous Provisions) (England) Regulations 2006 (SI 2006/373)).

- Properties occupied by two persons forming two households (Sch. 14, para. 7).

These exclusions operate as a jurisdictional gateway. If Schedule 14 applies, the property is not an HMO for the purposes of Part 2, and questions of mandatory or additional licensing do not arise.

HMOs required to be licensed

Where Part 2 does apply HMO must be licensed unless there is (a) a temporary exemption notice under section 62 or (b) an interim or final management order under Chapter 1, Part 4: section 61(1).

A licence under this Part is a licence authorising occupation of the house concerned by not more than a maximum number of households or persons specified in the licence: section 61(2).

By section 72(1), subject to certain statutory defences, a person commits a criminal offence if he is a person having control of or managing an HMO which is required to be licensed under this Part but is not so licensed. Operating a licensable HMO without a licence also exposes the relevant person to other potential enforcement action, including:

- the imposition of a civil penalty as an alternative to prosecution;

- liability to a rent repayment order; and
- restrictions on the service of certain notices seeking possession (see Chapter 10).

Section 61(4) imposes a duty on local housing authorities to take all reasonable steps to ensure that applications are made for HMOs in their area which are required to be licensed but are not. The duty is not, however, a duty to ensure that any particular landlord is aware of the scheme: see *Thanet DC v Grant* [2015] EWHC 4290 (Admin) on the equivalent provision in Part 3.

Temporary Exemption Notices

Section 62 makes provisions for temporary exemption notices. Section 62 makes provision for temporary exemption notices. By s.62(1), where a person having control of or managing an HMO which is required to be licensed but is not so licensed notifies the local housing authority of his intention to take particular steps with a view to securing that the house is no longer required to be licensed, the provisions of that section apply.

The authority may, if they think fit, serve a temporary exemption notice in respect of the house: section 62(2). While a valid notice is in force, the property is treated as not requiring a licence: section 62(3).

A temporary exemption notice has effect for a period of three months beginning with the date on which it is served (section 62(4)). A second notice may be served, but only where the authority receives a further notification under section 62(1) and considers that there are exceptional circumstances that justify a second notice taking effect from the end of the first three-month period. No further notice may be served beyond the second (section 62(5)). The exceptional circumstances condition is a meaningful threshold: an authority that does not accept the circumstances are exceptional may refuse the second notice, with the consequence that the person concerned faces criminal liability if the property remains unlicensed.

If the authority decide not to serve a temporary exemption notice, they must serve the person with a notice informing him of the decision, the reasons for it and the date on which it was made and inform him of the right to appeal to the tribunal within 28 days beginning with a date specified in the notice, which must be the date of the decision: section 62(6)-(7).

Such an appeal is by way of rehearing but matters of which the authority were unaware when they made their decision may be taken into account: section 62(8).

CHAPTER FOUR

ADDITIONAL LICENSING

Sections 56–60 of the Housing Act 2004 confer on local housing authorities a power to extend licensing requirements, beyond the mandatory licensing regime, to other categories of HMOs. This is known as 'additional licensing'.

Additional licensing remains confined to HMOs as defined by sections 254-259. Its purpose is to bring further categories of HMO within the licensing regime where evidence demonstrates systemic management problems in a defined locality.

The Power to Designate

Section 56(1) provides that a local housing authority may designate either the whole of its district or an area within it as subject to additional licensing in respect of a description of HMOs specified in the designation. The authority must therefore identify:

- the geographical area; and
- the class of HMOs to which licensing will apply.

The designation may be framed broadly. By virtue of section 56(4), it is permissible for the authority to extend licensing to all HMOs in the designated area, or to particular sub-categories defined by reference to occupation or structural characteristics.

Under section 56(2), the authority may make a designation only if it considers that a significant proportion of the HMOs of the relevant description in the area are being managed sufficiently ineffectively as to give rise, or to be likely to give rise, to one or more particular problems for occupiers or members of the public.

Before making a designation under section 56 the authority must ensure that it is consistent with the authority's overall housing strategy and forms part of a co-ordinated approach to tackling homelessness, empty properties and anti-social behaviour in the private rented sector (section 57(2)-(3)).

Section 57(4) requires the authority to consider whether other courses of action might provide an effective method of addressing the identified problems and to consider that making the designation will significantly assist in doing so.

Section 57(5) defines "anti-social behaviour" for the purposes of the Act as conduct on the part of occupiers of, or visitors to, residential premises which causes or is likely to cause nuisance or annoyance to persons residing, visiting or otherwise engaged in lawful activities in the vicinity, or which involves or is likely to involve the use of such premises for illegal purposes

Consultation

Section 56(3) requires the authority, before making a designation, to take reasonable steps to consult persons who are likely to be affected and to consider representations made and not withdrawn.

The category of persons likely to be affected is not confined to landlords within the designated area. In *R (Regas) v Enfield LBC* [2014] EWHC 4173 (Admin), the High Court held that residents and businesses in neighbouring boroughs fell within the consultation duty where displacement effects were foreseeable. The decision confirms that consultation must be lawful in scope and substance.

The statute itself does not prescribe a minimum consultation period. However, where a designation relies upon the General Approval 2024 (see below), the consultation must have been conducted for a period of not less than ten weeks. That requirement arises from the General Approval, not from section 56 itself.

Confirmation and the General Approval 2024

Under section 58(1), a designation cannot come into force unless it has been confirmed by the Secretary of State or falls within a description of designations for which a general approval has been given.

With effect from 23 December 2024, the General Approval 2024 provides standing approval for additional licensing designations in England, removing the need for individual confirmation provided certain conditions are met.

The principal condition is that the authority must have consulted under section 56(3)(a) for a period of not less than ten weeks prior to making the designation.

Where that condition is satisfied, and the other statutory requirements are met, the designation may come into force without separate Secretary of State confirmation. The designation must specify a commencement date not earlier than three months after it is made, in accordance with section 58(7)–(8).

If the ten-week consultation condition is not satisfied, the General Approval does not apply, and individual confirmation under section 58 would be required before the designation can take effect.

Authorities and practitioners must therefore verify both the existence of the General Approval and compliance with its conditions at the time of designation.

Notification

Once confirmed or validly made under the General Approval, the authority must publish notice in accordance with section 59 and the Licensing and Management of Houses in Multiple Occupation and Other Houses (Miscellaneous Provisions) (England) Regulations 2006.

The notice must describe the area, specify the commencement date, provide contact details, and warn that operating a licensable HMO without a licence is a criminal offence. Publication must be in prescribed forms, including local press and online.

Duration, Review, Revocation and Challenge

By section 60 a designation must specify its duration and may not exceed five years from commencement. The authority must review the operation of the designation from time to time and may revoke it where appropriate. Revocation must also be notified in the prescribed manner.

There is no statutory right of appeal against the making of an additional licensing designation. Challenge lies by way of judicial review.

CHAPTER FIVE

SELECTIVE LICENSING UNDER PART 3

Part 3 of the Housing Act 2004 establishes a licensing regime applicable to privately rented houses which are not already subject to licensing under Part 2. Unlike additional licensing, which is confined to HMOs, selective licensing may apply to single household dwellings let under assured tenancies or licences.

A house becomes subject to Part 3 only if a local housing authority makes a lawful designation under section 80. Once a designation comes into force, every "Part 3 house" within the designated area must be licensed unless an exemption applies (section 85(1)).

The regime is therefore area-based and designation-dependent.

The Power to Designate

Section 80(1) provides that a local housing authority may designate either the whole of its district or an area within it as subject to selective licensing if the requirements of subsections (2) and (9) are met.

The authority must consider that one of the statutory condition sets is satisfied (section 80(2)). The two primary statutory condition sets are low housing demand (section 80(3)); or significant and persistent anti-social behaviour (section 80(6)).

In addition, the appropriate national authority may specify further conditions by order under section 80(7). In England, this power has been exercised by the Selective Licensing of Houses (Additional Conditions) (England) Order 2015. In Wales, the equivalent instrument is The Selective Licensing of Houses (Additional Conditions) (Wales) Order 2016 (See below).

Selective licensing cannot apply to houses already required to be licensed under Part 2 (section 85(1)(a)).

The First Condition: Low Housing Demand

Under section 80(3), the first set of general conditions is satisfied where the area is, or is likely to become, an area of low housing demand; and making a designation will, when combined with other measures, contribute to improvement in the social or economic conditions of the area.

Section 80(4) specifies matters to which the authority must have regard in determining low housing demand, including: relative property values; turnover of occupiers; numbers and duration of vacant properties.

The statutory list is not exhaustive. The appropriate national authority may add further matters by order (section 80(5)).

The Second Condition: Anti-Social Behaviour

The second set of general conditions applies where the area is experiencing a significant and persistent problem caused by anti-social behaviour; some or all private sector landlords are failing to take appropriate action to combat that problem; and making the designation will, when combined with other measures, reduce or eliminate the problem (section 80(6)).

Anti-social behaviour" bears the definition in s.57(5): see Chapter 4.

It is notable that (1) The problem must be both significant and persistent and (2) There must be a failure by private landlords to take appropriate action. This introduces a landlord-responsibility element not present in the low-demand condition.

The High Court has confirmed that challenges to whether these statutory thresholds are met are reviewed on conventional public law principles: *R (Southern Landlords Association) v Thanet DC* [2012] EWHC 3187 (Admin).

Additional Conditions

Under section 80(7), further conditions may be specified by order. In England, the 2015 Order permits designation where the authority is satisfied that the area contains a high proportion of privately rented properties let under assured tenancies or licences; and one of four additional conditions is met, namely:

- the authority intends to inspect for Part 1 hazards;
- the area has experienced migration influx;
- the area suffers high levels of deprivation; or
- the area suffers high levels of crime.

In Wales, the 2016 Order prescribes additional designation conditions reflecting Welsh housing policy. Practitioners should note that Part 3 selective licensing operates alongside the separate landlord registration and licensing regime established under the Housing (Wales) Act 2014.

Further Considerations

Section 81 imposes further statutory requirements. The authority must ensure that the designation is consistent with its overall housing strategy (section 81(2)); and it forms part of a co-ordinated approach to homelessness, empty properties and anti-social behaviour (section 81(3)).

Before designating, the authority must consider whether other courses of action might achieve the objective; and consider that designation will significantly assist in achieving it (section 81(4)).

There is no prohibition on designating where other options exist. The authority may conclude that licensing remains appropriate even if alternatives are available. Any challenge is assessed on conventional Wednesbury principles: *R (Rotherham Action Group Ltd) v Rotherham MBC* [2015] EWHC 1216 (Admin).

Consultation

Before making a designation, the authority must take reasonable steps to consult persons likely to be affected and consider representations made and not withdrawn (section 80(9)).

"Reasonable steps" does not mean exhaustive consultation. In *R (Croydon Property Forum Ltd) v Croydon LBC* [2015] EWHC 2403 (Admin), targeted landlord mailings and public publicity were sufficient.

Consultation may extend beyond borough boundaries where displacement effects are foreseeable: *R (Regas) v Enfield LBC* [2014] EWHC 4173 (Admin).

Where reliance is placed on the General Approval 2024, consultation must have lasted not less than ten weeks.

Confirmation or General Approval

Under section 82, a designation cannot come into force unless confirmed by the Secretary of State; or falling within a description of designations subject to general approval.

As with additional licensing the General Approval 2024, in force in England from 23 December 2024, grants standing approval provided consultation lasted at least ten weeks.

The designation must specify a commencement date not earlier than three months after confirmation or making (section82(4), (8)).

Once in force, Part 3 applies to occupation even if that occupation began before designation (section 82(9)).

Notification

By section 83, following confirmation or making, the authority must publish notice in the prescribed manner, stating that the designation has been made whether confirmation or general approval applied and the commencement date.

The authority must also make copies of the designation publicly available while it remains in force.

Failure to comply with notification requirements may render the designation vulnerable to challenge.

Duration and Review

A designation must specify its duration and cannot exceed five years from commencement.

The authority must review its operation from time to time and may revoke it where appropriate.

Revocation must be notified in the prescribed manner (section 84)

Requirement to Licence

By section 85 once designation takes effect, every Part 3 house must be licensed unless:

- it is subject to Part 2 licensing;
- a temporary exemption notice is in force (section 86); or
- a management order applies.

The authority must take reasonable steps to secure that applications are made (section 85(4)). This is not a duty to ensure every landlord is personally aware of the scheme: *Thanet DC v Grant* (Divisional Court, 2015).

Temporary Exemption Notices

Where a person having control or managing a Part 3 house notifies the authority of steps to secure that it will cease to require licensing, the authority may serve a temporary exemption notice: section 86. Such notice lasts three months and may be extended once, in exceptional circumstances, for a further three months.

If refused, the applicant has a right of appeal to the First-tier Tribunal within 28 days.

CHAPTER SIX

LANDLORD REGISTRATION AND LICENSING IN WALES

Part 1 of the Housing (Wales) Act 2014 introduced a mandatory national system of landlord registration and licensing in Wales.

Mandatory HMO licensing, additional HMO licensing and selective licensing under Housing Act 2004 continues to apply in Wales. The 2014 Act adds an additional person-based regulatory layer governing who may carry out letting and management activities.

A landlord in Wales may therefore require a property licence under the Housing Act 2004; and registration and, where applicable, a landlord licence under the 2014 Act.

Section 1 of the 2014 Act provides that Part 1 regulates the letting and management of dwellings subject to "domestic tenancies" by means of registration and licensing.

The Welsh Ministers have designated Cardiff Council as the licensing authority, which administers the scheme under the banner "Rent Smart Wales" for all 22 local authorities in Wales.

The scheme has three principal elements:

a) Mandatory registration of all private landlords in respect of each rental property (sections 4–5, 14–17);

b) Licensing of landlords who carry out letting or management activities (sections 6–8, 18–26);

c) Licensing of agents who carry out lettings work or property management work (sections 9–13).

A "rental property" is a dwelling which is subject to, or is marketed or offered for let under, a domestic tenancy (section 2). The regime therefore applies not only to occupied properties but also to those being advertised. Although Part 1 retains the terminology of "domestic tenancy", it now applies to occupation contracts within the meaning of the Renting Homes (Wales) Act 2016, subject to the statutory exclusions in section 2.

Registration of Landlords

Under section 4, the landlord of a rental property must be registered in respect of that dwelling unless an exception applies. Failure to register without reasonable excuse is a criminal offence (section 4(3)).

Registration is required whether or not the landlord personally undertakes management functions.

The licensing authority must maintain a register (section 14). An application must be made in the prescribed form, include prescribed information and the appropriate fee (section 15). Registration is largely administrative. There is no statutory fit and proper person test at the registration stage.

A registered landlord must notify the authority of prescribed changes in circumstances within 28 days (section 16). Registration may be revoked in prescribed circumstances (section 17), subject to a right of appeal.

Licensing of Landlords

Registration alone does not entitle a landlord to carry out regulated activities.

Section 6 prohibits a landlord from carrying out specified lettings activities unless licensed or acting through a licensed agent. These activities include arranging viewings, gathering evidence of tenant suitability, preparing tenancy agreements and inventories.

Breach is an offence (section 6(3)).

Section 7 prohibits a landlord from carrying out specified property management activities unless licensed or acting through a licensed agent.

Property management activities include collecting rent, arranging repairs, inspecting the dwelling and, importantly, serving notice to terminate a tenancy or occupation contract (section 7(2)).

Carrying out such activity without a licence is a criminal offence (s.7(5)).

Fit and Proper Person Test

An application for a landlord licence must comply with section 19. The licensing authority must grant a licence if satisfied that the applicant is a fit and proper person and has completed prescribed training (section 20).

Section 20(3) requires the authority to have regard to matters including:

- convictions involving fraud, violence, drugs or sexual offences;

- unlawful discrimination;
- contraventions of housing law;
- previous licence breaches;
- the conduct of associated persons.

Under section 20(6), the Welsh Ministers must issue guidance to which authorities must have regard. The guidance emphasises that the purpose of the test is tenant protection. It makes clear that:

- both spent and unspent convictions may be relevant where they indicate risk;
- there is no automatic exclusion;
- patterns of non-compliance may be as significant as individual offences;
- associated persons, including company directors or partners, may be relevant;
- safeguarding and equality considerations are central.

Training is a mandatory component of licensing. Refusal or failure to complete approved training may indicate unsuitability.

Licences are granted for five years (section 26) unless revoked or surrendered.

Licensing of Agents

Sections 9 and 11 require agents carrying out lettings work or property management work to be licensed.

"Lettings work" and "property management work" are defined in sections 10 and 12 and broadly mirror the activities prohibited to unlicensed landlords.

Section 13 makes it an offence for a landlord to appoint or continue to allow an unlicensed person to carry out such work where the landlord knows or ought to know of the absence of a licence.

Parallel liability may therefore arise for both landlord and agent.

Restriction on Serving Notices to Recover Possession

A significant consequence of non-compliance concerns possession proceedings. Because serving notice to terminate a tenancy or occupation contract constitutes property management work (section 7(2)), an unlicensed landlord who serves such a notice commits an offence under section 7(5).

Section 44 (as amended) provides that specified termination notices under the Renting Homes (Wales) Act 2016 may not be given where the landlord is not registered or, where required, not licensed (or has not appointed a licensed agent for all property management work). The provision applies, in particular, to notices under section 173 and other statutory termination mechanisms under the 2016 Act. Compliance with the registration and licensing regime is therefore a precondition to lawful recovery of possession.

Enforcement Overview

Part 1 of the 2014 Act creates criminal offences for failure to register, failure to obtain a licence when required, and appointing unlicensed agents. Fixed penalty notices may be issued as an alternative to prosecution (section 29).

The Act also provides for rent stopping orders (section 30) and rent repayment orders (sections 32–33). The rent repayment provisions are considered separately in Chapter 12.

PART II

LICENSING PROCEDURE AND LIABILITY

CHAPTER SEVEN

APPLICATIONS, GRANT, VARIATION, REVOCATION AND APPEALS

Once it has been established that a property requires a licence under Part 2 (mandatory or additional HMO licensing) or under Part 3 (selective licensing), the procedural machinery in sections 63–71 and sections 87–94 of the Housing Act 2004 applies. Although Parts 2 and 3 are not identical, the structure governing application, determination, variation, revocation and appeal is materially parallel and must be read together with Schedule 5.

An application for a Part 2 licence must be made to the local housing authority under section 63(1). Section 63(2) provides that the application must comply with such requirements as the authority may specify, but that power is expressly subject to regulations made under section 63(5). The Licensing and Management of Houses in Multiple Occupation and Other Houses (Miscellaneous Provisions) Regulations 2006 prescribe the information that must accompany an application, including details of the proposed licence holder and manager, declarations relating to safety and relevant convictions, and notification to persons with estates or interests in the property. The authority's discretion to "specify requirements" is therefore constrained by those Regulations.

The limits of that discretion were considered in *R (Gaskin) v Richmond upon Thames LBC* [2018] EWHC 1996 (Admin); [2018] H.L.R. 47. The High Court held that the statutory scheme under Part 2 constitutes an authorisation regime and that the prescribed information requirements are exhaustive. An authority may not impose additional mandatory information requirements beyond those permitted by section 63 and the Regulations. The reasoning applies equally to selective licensing applications under section 87.

Sections 63(3) and 87(3) permit the authority to require payment of a licence fee. Sections 63(7) and 87(7) provide that, in fixing the amount of the fee, the authority may take into account costs incurred in carrying out functions under the relevant Part and certain management order functions under Part 4. However, *Gaskin* confirms that, as an authorisation scheme, the fee required at the application stage must be confined to the cost of the authorisation procedures and formalities. It is not lawful to require, upfront, payment that includes wider enforcement or scheme-running costs. Authorities commonly structure licence fees to reflect that distinction. Where it transpires that a property did not require a licence, the Regulations require that the fee be refunded.

Under section 64(1), in the Part 2 context, the authority must either grant or refuse the licence. Section 88(1) imposes the same obligation in relation to Part 3 selective licensing. The authority has no power to leave an application undetermined. Section 64(3) provides that a licence may be granted only if the authority is satisfied that the house is reasonably suitable for occupation by not more than the maximum number specified (or can be made so by licence conditions), that no banning order is in force against a relevant person, that the proposed licence holder is a fit and proper person and the most appropriate person reasonably available, that any proposed manager is fit and proper, and that the management arrangements are satisfactory. The parallel requirements are found in section 88 in Part 3.

Suitability for occupation is addressed further in section 65 (Part 2), which provides that the authority cannot be satisfied as to suitability if prescribed standards are not met. Those standards are set out in the 2006 Regulations and concern facilities, amenities and safety measures. Even where prescribed standards are met, the authority retains discretion to conclude that the house is not reasonably suitable for the proposed level of occupation. The assessment is evaluative but must be grounded in the statutory criteria.

The "fit and proper person" test under section 66 (Part 2) and section 89 (Part 3) is central. In determining fitness, the authority must have regard to evidence that the person has committed offences involving fraud, dishonesty, violence, drugs or certain sexual offences; practised unlawful discrimination; or contravened housing or landlord and tenant law. The statutory list is non-exhaustive, and the assessment is forward-looking and protective.

In *Hussain v London Borough of Waltham Forest* [2020] EWCA Civ 1539; [2021] 1 WLR 922 the Court of Appeal considered the interaction between section 66 and the Rehabilitation of Offenders Act 1974. The Court held that section 4(1)(a) of the 1974 Act renders inadmissible evidence of the fact of a spent conviction, but does not render inadmissible the conduct underlying that conviction. The underlying conduct may therefore be considered in licensing proceedings. The Court further indicated that a local housing authority determining a licence application under Parts 2 or 3 is a "judicial authority" for the purposes of section 4(6) of the 1974 Act and may rely on section 7(3) where justice cannot otherwise be done.

Planning irregularities may also be relevant. In *Waltham Forest LBC v Khan* [2017] UKUT 153 (LC), the Upper Tribunal confirmed that planning status may legitimately be taken into account when determining the duration or terms of a licence. Licensing and planning are distinct regulatory regimes, but they operate within the same factual context and are not mutually irrelevant.

Licences may not exceed five years in duration under section 68 (Part 2) and section 91 (Part 3). Duration is a matter of evaluative judgment. In *Waltham Forest LBC v Reid* [2017] UKUT 396 (LC), the Upper Tribunal held that although previous convictions were relevant to the length of a licence, a one-year licence imposed on the facts was unjustified. The purpose of duration is regulatory control, not punishment.

Variation is governed by section 69 (Part 2) and section 92 (Part 3). A licence may be varied with the agreement of the licence holder or, without agreement, where there has been a change of circumstances. Revocation is governed by section 70 (Part 2) and section 93 (Part 3), including cases of serious or repeated breach, loss of fitness, or cessation of licensable status. Where a banning order is made, revocation becomes mandatory under sections 70A and 93A.

Appeals are governed by Schedule 5. Decisions to refuse, grant with conditions, vary, revoke or refuse a temporary exemption notice are appealable to the First-tier Tribunal (Property Chamber) in England and the Residential Property Tribunal in Wales. The appeal must be lodged within 28 days, subject to the Tribunal's power to extend time.

The nature of the appeal was clarified by the Court of Appeal in *Waltham Forest LBC v Hussain* [2023] EWCA Civ 733; [2023] H.L.R. 40. Although described as a rehearing, the Tribunal's task is to determine whether the authority's decision was wrong at the time it was made. It is not a wholly fresh merits determination divorced from the original decision. Subsequent evidence may be admitted, but only insofar as it assists in determining whether the original decision was wrong. Earlier authority, including *Brent LBC v Reynolds* [2001] EWCA Civ 1843, indicates that tribunals should pay careful attention to the authority's evaluative judgment.

The sequencing of application, determination and enforcement is critical. Sections 72(4) (Part 2) and 95(3) (Part 3) provide that a person does not commit the offence of having control of or managing an unlicensed property if a duly made application for a licence is outstanding. The statutory scheme therefore contemplates that an application must be determined before criminal liability for operating without a licence can arise. Sections 64(1) and 88(1) impose a duty on the authority to grant or refuse an application; they do not permit indefinite deferral. In principle, the institution of criminal proceedings while a valid application remains undetermined may give rise to arguments of procedural unfairness or abuse of process.

CHAPTER EIGHT

WHO IS RESPONSIBLE?

Criminal liability for operating a licensable property without a licence arises under section 72(1) of the Housing Act 2004 in relation to Part 2 (mandatory and additional HMO licensing), and under section 95(1) in relation to Part 3 (selective licensing). In each case, the offence is committed by a person who has control of or manages a house which is required to be licensed but is not so licensed.

The expressions "*person having control*" and "*person managing*" are defined in section 263 of the 2004 Act. Those definitions apply across Parts 1 to 4 and must be applied strictly. Liability does not depend upon who is colloquially described as "*the landlord*", nor upon contractual labels adopted by the parties. It depends upon whether the factual matrix satisfies the statutory elements.

Section 263(1) provides that a person has control of premises if they receive the rack-rent of the premises, whether on their own account or as agent or trustee of another, or if they would receive the rack-rent if the premises were let at a rack-rent. "*Rack-rent*" is defined in section 263(2) as rent not less than two-thirds of the full net annual value of the premises.

It is not necessary, as a matter of law, for rack-rent to be established by expert valuation evidence in every case. In appropriate circumstances, the terms of the occupation arrangements themselves may provide sufficient evidential foundation. In *Global 100 Ltd v Jimenez* [2023] EWCA Civ 1243, the Court of Appeal upheld the tribunal's conclusion that the aggregate licence payments received from property guardians (approximately £15,000 per month) were capable of evidencing the rack-rent of the premises. The company was operating commercially and was not a charitable body. The tribunal was entitled to infer that the premises were being let on the best available terms and that the sums actually received reflected their net annual value.

Identification of the person in receipt of rack-rent will frequently be central to the analysis of control under section 263(1): *Cottam v Lowe Management Ltd* [2023] UKUT 306 (LC). The question is not merely who participates in the management structure, but who is legally entitled to the economic return from the premises.

Section 263(3) defines a "person managing" as the person who, being an owner or lessee of the premises, either (a) receives rents or other payments from persons who are in occupation as tenants or licensees of parts of the premises or, in the case of a Part 3 house, of parts or the whole of the premises or (b) would so receive those rents or payments but for having entered into an arrangement with another person who is not an owner or lessee by virtue of which that other person receives them instead. Where rents or payments are received through an agent or trustee, that agent or trustee is also included within the definition.

In *Cetin v Epping Forest DC* [2025] UKUT 196 (LC), the Upper Tribunal emphasised that the definition of "*person managing*" in section 263(3) is directed at those who assume substantive management responsibility for the premises. Although the statutory language refers to receipt of rent, receipt is treated as an indicator of management status rather than an end in itself. The provision is concerned with continuing responsibility. An agent whose role was limited to introducing a tenant and receiving a single payment, without any ongoing management duties, did not fall within the definition.

That approach was reinforced in *Next Location Co Ltd v Haringey LBC* [2025] UKUT 279 (LC) where the Tribunal held that a person who receives no rent or other payment from occupiers cannot satisfy section 263(3).

Where the person identified as having control or managing is a body corporate, section 251 provides that directors, managers, secretaries or similar officers are also guilty of the offence if it is proved to have been committed with their consent or connivance, or attributable to their neglect. Liability under section 251 is derivative and requires proof of the underlying corporate offence.

The same identification exercise under section 263 underpins both criminal prosecution and the imposition of civil penalties under section 249A, which requires the authority to be satisfied beyond reasonable doubt that a relevant housing offence has been committed.

CHAPTER NINE

LICENCE CONDITIONS

A licence granted under Part 2 (mandatory or additional HMO licensing) or Part 3 (selective licensing) authorises occupation of the house subject to compliance with specified conditions. Licence conditions are the principal regulatory mechanism through which standards of management, safety and amenity are imposed and enforced.

The starting point is Schedule 4 to the Housing Act 2004, which is headed "Licences Under Parts 2 and 3: Mandatory Conditions". Paragraph 1(1) of Schedule 4 provides that a licence under Part 2 or Part 3 must include the conditions set out in that Schedule. Schedule 4 therefore applies equally to HMO licences and selective licences. It is not a Part 2-only instrument.

Beyond those mandatory conditions, the discretionary powers to impose further conditions differ materially between Part 2 and Part 3, and that difference is of practical and legal significance.

Mandatory Conditions: Schedule 4

Because Schedule 4 operates across both licensing regimes, its provisions are conveniently addressed together before turning to the distinct discretionary powers under each Part.

Gas safety. Where gas is supplied to the house, the licence must require the licence holder to produce to the local housing authority annually a gas safety certificate obtained within the previous twelve months

(Sch. 4, para. 1(2)). This obligation applies in both England and Wales under both Parts.

Electrical appliances and furniture. The licence must require the licence holder to keep electrical appliances and furniture made available by them in a safe condition, and to supply the authority on demand with a declaration as to their safety (Sch. 4, para. 1(3)(a)–(b)). This applies in both jurisdictions under both Parts. In England only, an additional requirement applies: the licence must also require the licence holder to ensure that every electrical installation in the house is in proper working order and safe for continued use, and to supply a declaration as to its safety on demand (Sch. 4, para. 1(3)(c)–(d), inserted by SI 2020/312).

Smoke alarms. The provision differs between England and Wales. In England, the licence must require the licence holder to ensure that a smoke alarm is installed on each storey on which there is a room used wholly or partly as living accommodation, and to keep each alarm in proper working order (Sch. 4, para. 1(4)(za), inserted by SI 2015/1693). In Wales, the requirement is framed more broadly: the licence must require that smoke alarms are installed in the house and kept in proper working order (Sch. 4, para. 1(4)(a)). In both jurisdictions the licence must require the holder to supply a declaration as to the condition and positioning of the alarms on demand (Sch. 4, para. 1(4)(b)).

Carbon monoxide alarms. In England only, the licence must require the licence holder to ensure that a carbon monoxide alarm is installed in any room used wholly or partly as living accommodation which contains a fixed combustion appliance other than a gas cooker, to keep any such alarm in proper working order, and to supply a declaration as to its condition and positioning on demand (Sch. 4, para. 1(4A), as amended by SI 2022/707). Wales has adopted its own carbon monoxide alarm requirements through separate Welsh regulations operating alongside licensing.

Written statement of occupation terms. The licence must require the licence holder to supply to the occupiers of the house a written statement of the terms on which they occupy it (Sch. 4, para. 1(5)). This applies under both Parts in both jurisdictions. In Wales, this requirement now operates alongside the statutory obligation to provide written statements of occupation contracts under the Renting Homes (Wales) Act 2016.

Definitions. In England, para. 1(6) provides that for the purposes of para. 1(4A), "room" includes a hall or landing. Paragraph 1(7) provides that for the purposes of paras. 1(4) and 1(4A), a bathroom or lavatory is to be treated as a room used as living accommodation. These definitional provisions are England-specific.

Discretionary Conditions: Part 2 (HMO Licensing)

Beyond the mandatory Schedule 4 conditions, section 67 governs the imposition of further conditions in Part 2 licences. Section 67(1) confers a broad discretion: a licence may include such conditions as the authority considers appropriate for regulating "all or any of the following - (a) the management, use and occupation of the house concerned, and (b) its condition and contents."

The inclusion of limb (b), condition and content, is of direct importance. It confirms that under Part 2 a local housing authority may impose conditions relating to the physical state of the property and its contents, including the provision and maintenance of facilities and equipment. Section 67(2) makes this explicit by listing in its "in particular" provisions conditions requiring facilities and equipment to be made available to meet prescribed standards (section 67(2)(c)), kept in repair and working order (section 67(2)(d)), and provided within specified timescales (section 67(2)(e)).

Non-exhaustive examples of the discretionary power under section 67(2) include restrictions on the use of particular parts of the house, requirements to take reasonable and practicable steps to prevent or reduce anti-social behaviour, and requirements to attend training relating to approved codes of practice under section 233. Authorities may also impose time limits for works and requirements concerning the adequacy of facilities and amenities.

The discretion must be exercised lawfully and for the statutory purpose. Conditions must be rational, proportionate and directed at regulation of the property and its management. In *Nottingham City Council v Parr* [2018] UKSC 51, the Supreme Court confirmed that conditions restricting occupation to particular categories of occupier, such as full-time students, may lawfully be imposed within the statutory framework.

Discretionary Conditions: Part 3 (Selective Licensing)

The discretionary power under Part 3 is materially narrower than under Part 2, and the difference is deliberate.

Section 90(1) provides that a licence may include such conditions as the authority considers appropriate for regulating "the management, use or occupation of the house concerned." Conspicuously absent from section 90(1), by contrast with section 67(1), is any reference to the condition or contents of the house.

The significance of that omission was authoritatively resolved by the Court of Appeal in *Brown v Hyndburn Borough Council* [2018] EWCA Civ 242; [2018] 1 WLR 4518. The local housing authority had imposed conditions on a selective licence requiring the installation of a carbon monoxide detector and the provision of a valid electrical installation condition report. The Court of Appeal held that both conditions were outside the authority's powers under section 90(1). The word "management" in that provision, read alongside "use or occupation" and in the knowledge that, unlike section 67(1), section 90(1) says nothing about condition, contents, facilities or equipment, connotes operational matters: what actually happens at and to the property. Ensuring rubbish is properly presented for collection, keeping fire escapes clear, or promptly re-glazing broken windows may fall within it. Requiring the installation of new equipment or the improvement of installations to a prescribed standard does not.

Section 90(2) identifies two particular instances of the section 90(1) power: conditions restricting use or occupation of particular parts of the house, and conditions requiring steps to prevent or reduce anti-social behaviour. Both are operational in character, consistent with the analysis above.

Conditions relating to facilities and equipment are authorised separately under section 90(3), which is prefaced by "also" precisely because such conditions fall outside section 90(1). The section 90(3) power is however conditional on the existence of standards prescribed by regulations made by the appropriate national authority, and no such regulations have been made. That route therefore remains currently unavailable, leaving Schedule 4 as the only basis on which conditions of that character may be included in a selective licence.

Section 90(5) is not a further source of power. It addresses the relationship between the authority's licensing functions and its Part 1 functions, requiring the authority generally to address category 1 and 2 hazards through Part 1 enforcement rather than licence conditions, whilst preserving the ability to impose conditions under section 90(3) even where Part 1 could achieve the same result. The Court of Appeal in Brown v Hyndburn confirmed that section 90(5) confers no residual discretion to impose conditions beyond those authorised by section 90(1) and section 90(3).

The overarching principle is that improving housing standards is primarily the function of Part 1 and, for HMOs, Part 2. Part 3 licensing is directed at management, use and occupation of private sector accommodation as it affects the locality- addressing low housing demand and anti-social behaviour. Discretionary conditions must be appropriate to that purpose.

Statutory Limits Applicable to Both Parts

Section 67(5) (Part 2) and s.90(6) (Part 3) provide that a licence may not impose restrictions or obligations on a person other than the licence holder without that person's consent. Section 67(6) (Part 2) and s.90(7) (Part 3) provide that a licence may not include conditions requiring, or intended to secure, any alteration in the terms of a tenancy or licence under which a person occupies the house.

Relationship with Part 1 (HHSRS)

The interaction between licence conditions and enforcement under Part 1 is governed by section 67(4) (Part 2) and section 90(5) (Part 3). In general, category 1 and category 2 hazards should be addressed through the exercise of Part 1 functions rather than through licence conditions. However, the imposition of licence conditions does not prevent subsequent exercise of Part 1 powers, and the authority is not prevented from imposing conditions under section 67(2) (Part 2) or section 90(3) (Part 3) relating to installation or maintenance of facilities even where similar matters could be addressed under Part 1. Licensing and HHSRS enforcement operate in parallel.

Breach of Conditions

Failure without reasonable excuse to comply with a licence condition constitutes a criminal offence under section 72(3) (Part 2) or section 95(3) (Part 3). In both jurisdictions the authority may alternatively impose a financial penalty under section 249A where satisfied beyond reasonable doubt that the offence has been committed. Breach may also justify variation or revocation of the licence under sections 69–70 (Part 2) or sections 92–93 (Part 3).

PART III

CRIMINAL AND CIVIL ENFORCEMENT

CHAPTER TEN

CRIMINAL OFFENCES AND PROSECUTION

The licensing regimes under Parts 2 and 3 of the Housing Act 2004 are enforced through criminal offences. Although civil penalties are now widely used, the statutory scheme remains criminal at its core. The offence provisions define when operating a licensable property becomes unlawful and provide the basis for further consequences such as rent repayment orders and banning orders.

This chapter addresses the offences, the identification of the responsible person, available defences, and sentencing.

The Offences: HMOS

A person commits an offence if he has control of or manages an HMO which is required to be licensed but is not so licensed (section 72(1)). The offence is one of strict liability. The prosecution is not required to prove that the defendant knew the property was an HMO or that it required a licence (*R (Mohamed) v Waltham Forest LBC* [2020] EWHC 1083 (Admin)).

A person commits an offence if he knowingly permits occupation in excess of the number authorised by a licence (section 72(2)). The prosecution must establish that the defendant knowingly permitted occupation beyond the authorised number. Knowledge means actual knowledge, although deliberate blindness may suffice (*R v Hallam* [1957] 1 QB 569; *Warner v Metropolitan Police Commissioner* [1969] 2 AC 256). Mere negligence is insufficient.

A defence is available under section 76(2) where excess occupiers were already in occupation when the licence came into force, provided the defendant was taking all reasonable steps to reduce occupation to the permitted number.

A licence holder also commits an offence if he fails, without reasonable excuse, to comply with a licence condition (s.72(3)).

The offences under s.72(1) and s.72(2) are summary only and punishable by an unlimited fine (s.72(6)). The offence under s.72(3) (breach of licence condition) is also summary only but carries a maximum fine not exceeding level 5 on the standard scale (s.72(7)).

Selective Licensing

A person commits an offence if he has control of or manages a house required to be licensed under Part 3 but which is not so licensed (section 95(1)).

The offence under section 95(1), like section 72(1), is one of strict liability. The prosecution is not required to prove that the defendant knew the property required a licence. The structure of the provision mirrors section 72 and is interpreted consistently.

A licence holder commits an offence if he fails to comply with a licence condition (section 95(2)). A person other than the licence holder may also be liable where restrictions or obligations have been imposed upon him under section 90(6).

The offence under s.95(1) (unlicensed operation) is summary only and punishable by an unlimited fine (s.95(5)). The offence under s.95(2) (breach of licence condition) is also summary only but carries a maximum fine not exceeding level 5 on the standard scale (s.95(6)).

Confiscation under the Proceeds of Crime Act 2002 is not available in respect of rent received during the unlicensed period, as rent is not obtained "as a result of" criminal conduct: *Sumal & Sons (Properties) Ltd v LB Newham* [2012] EWCA Crim 1840.

Who Is Liable?

Liability depends on the definitions of "person having control" and "person managing" in section 263. A person has control if he receives the rack-rent, or would receive it if the premises were let at a rack-rent (section 263(1)). A person managing includes an owner or lessee who receives rents from occupiers or who would receive them but for a diversion arrangement (section 263(3)). See further Chapter 8.

Corporate officers may be liable where the offence was committed with their consent or connivance, or attributable to their neglect: section 251(1).

When is an offence committed?

Proceedings must ordinarily be commenced within six months of the commission of the offence (Magistrates' Courts Act 1980, section 127).

An offence under section 72(1) or section 95(1) is a continuing offence and is committed afresh on each day that the property remains unlicensed (*Luton BC v Altavon Luton Ltd* [2019] EWHC 2415 (Admin)).

Where a defendant relies on reasonable excuse, the reasonableness of the excuse must be assessed throughout the whole period during which the offence is committed (*Marigold v Wells* [2023] UKUT 33 (LC)).

Defences

No offence is committed where, at the material time, a duly made notification or application was outstanding and effective (section 72(4); section 95(3)). In the Part 3 context this includes notification under section 86(1) (temporary exemption notices for Part 3 houses).

A notification or application is "effective" if it has not been withdrawn and either the authority has not yet decided whether to grant the licence or serve the notice, or (if it has refused) the period for appealing has not expired or any appeal has not been determined (section 95(7)–(9); Sch 5).

An application may be "duly made" even where the authority has failed to process it or where technical issues arise with an online portal, provided the defendant can show genuine attempts to apply (*Fashade v Albustin* [2023] UKUT 40 (LC); *Chong v Severgnini* [2024] UKUT 348 (LC)).

There is also a defence of "reasonable excuse" (section 72(5); section 95(4)). The scope of "reasonable excuse" has been considered extensively in the Upper Tribunal. Reliance on misleading information from a local authority website may, in principle, amount to a reasonable excuse (*Ojukwu v Onuoha* [2024] UKUT 313 (LC)). Reliance on an agent may suffice only where the agent had a contractual responsibility for licensing and the landlord was reasonably entitled to rely on their competence (*Aytan v Moore* [2022] UKUT 27 (LC)).

By contrast, failure to investigate the licensing position on purchase will not ordinarily amount to a reasonable excuse (*Gateshead MBC v City Estate Holdings Ltd* [2023] UKUT 35 (LC)). Large commercial operators cannot shift responsibility to the authority for failing to alert them to licensing requirements (*LDC (Ferry Lane) GP3 Ltd v Garro* [2024] UKUT 40 (LC)).

Sentencing

The maximum fine for operating an unlicensed property is unlimited (s.72(6); s.95(5)). Breach of a licence condition carries a lower maximum of level 5 on the standard scale (s.72(7); s.95(6)). This distinction is significant in practice: where enforcement is directed at a persistent failure to licence, the unlimited fine provision applies; where the charge is non-compliance with a specific condition, the level 5 cap governs.

There are currently no offence-specific sentencing guideline for offences under sections 72 or 95.

Generally, fines for individuals are calculated by reference to relevant weekly income. The court selects a fine band based on culpability and harm, applies a percentage of weekly income, and adjusts for aggravating and mitigating factors and plea. For organisations, fines are assessed by reference to turnover and financial circumstances, applying regulatory sentencing principles of proportionality and deterrence.

However, at the time of writing the Sentencing Council is consulting on proposed offence-specific sentencing guidelines for housing offences, including offences under sections 72 and 95. The proposed guideline would introduce structured harm and culpability categories and defined starting points and ranges. It would address factors such as overcrowding, fire risk, vulnerability of occupiers, and financial gain.

Relationship with Civil Penalties

A local housing authority may impose a civil financial penalty as an alternative to prosecution section 249A (see Chapter 10). If a civil penalty is imposed, the person may not be convicted of the same offence (section 72(7A); section 95(6A)).

CHAPTER ELEVEN

CIVIL PENALTIES

Civil penalties under section 249A of the Housing Act 2004 represent a substantial development in the enforcement landscape. Introduced by the Housing and Planning Act 2016, they permit a local housing authority ("LHA") to impose a financial penalty as an alternative to prosecution for specified housing offences. The underlying offences remain criminal. The civil penalty regime does not decriminalise them; it provides a procedurally distinct but substantively punitive enforcement route.

Section 249A(1) provides that an LHA may impose a financial penalty if satisfied, beyond reasonable doubt, that a person's conduct amounts to a "relevant housing offence" in respect of premises in England. The criminal standard of proof therefore applies. The authority must be satisfied that, were the matter prosecuted in the magistrates' court, there would be a realistic prospect of conviction. The April 2018 statutory guidance confirms that authorities should apply the evidential and public interest stages in the Code for Crown Prosecutors by analogy.

The "relevant housing offences" are exhaustively defined in section 249A(2). They include offences under section 30 (failure to comply with an improvement notice), section 72 (licensing of HMOs), section 95 (licensing of houses under Part 3), section 139(7) (contravention of overcrowding notice), and section 234 (breach of HMO management regulations). Only one financial penalty may be imposed in respect of the same conduct (section 249A(3)), and the maximum penalty is £30,000 (section 249A(4)). A civil penalty cannot be imposed if the person has already been convicted of the offence or if criminal proceedings have been instituted and not concluded (section 249A(5)). The election between prosecution and civil penalty must therefore be made at the outset and adhered to.

The procedural framework is contained in Schedule 13A to the 2004 Act. Before imposing a financial penalty, the authority must serve a Notice of Intent (Sch.13A, para.1). The Notice must be given before the end of the period of six months beginning with the first day on which the authority has sufficient evidence of the conduct to which the penalty relates (Sch.13A, para.2(1)). Where the conduct is continuing, the Notice may be given at any time while it continues, or within six months of the last day of the conduct (Sch.13A, para.2(2)). "Conduct" expressly includes a failure to act (Sch.13A, para.2(3)). The question of when the authority first had "sufficient evidence" is often central to limitation arguments and requires careful factual analysis.

The Notice of Intent must state the amount of the proposed penalty, the reasons for proposing to impose it, and information about the right to make representations (Sch.13A, para.3). The recipient has 28 days, beginning with the day after service, in which to make written representations (Sch.13A, para.4(2)). After that period, the authority must decide whether to impose a penalty and, if so, its amount (Sch.13A, para.5). If it decides to proceed, it must serve a Final Notice (Sch.13A, para.6) requiring payment within 28 days beginning with the day after service (Sch.13A, para.7). The Final Notice must set out the amount, the reasons, payment details, appeal rights and the consequences of non-payment (Sch.13A, para.8). The authority retains power to withdraw the Notice of Intent or Final Notice, or to reduce the amount, at any time (Sch.13A, para.9).

The drafting of Notices requires the same care as the framing of criminal charges. In *Majaraj v Liverpool City Council* [2022] UKUT 140 (LC), the Upper Tribunal quashed a financial penalty where the conduct described in the notice did not in fact constitute a breach of the relevant licence condition. Conversely, the Upper Tribunal has emphasised that a Notice of Intent is to be assessed by reference to how it would be understood by a reasonable reader. In *London Borough of Waltham Forest v Younis* [2019] UKUT 339 (LC); [2020] H.L.R. 17, the Tribunal held that a notice was not invalid merely because it did not set out in detail the calculation of the proposed penalty, provided that, read fairly and in context, it identified the alleged breach and its seriousness. Section 233 of the Local Government Act 1972 applies to service: see *Newcastle City Council v Abdallah* [2024] UKUT 140 (LC).

The amount of the penalty is a matter for the authority, subject to the £30,000 cap. The statutory guidance identifies a series of factors to be taken into account, including the severity of the offence, the culpability and track record of the offender, the harm caused or risked, the need for punishment and deterrence, and the removal of financial benefit. The maximum should be reserved for the worst offenders. Authorities are expected to adopt and publish their own policies on quantum. Where such a policy exists, the First-tier Tribunal should pay close attention to it and should be slow to depart from it without good reason: *Waltham Forest LBC v Marshall and Ustek* [2020] UKUT 35 (LC).

The Upper Tribunal has provided guidance on the proper approach to quantum. The penalty must reflect the harm caused by the offence which gives rise to liability. In *AA Homes & Housing Ltd and Anabow Services Ltd v Croydon LBC* [2020] UKUT 181 (LC), the Tribunal held that it was wrong to increase the penalty for a licensing offence by reference to unrelated fire safety defects. Investigatory costs cannot be added to the penalty: *Leicester City Council v Morjaria* [2023] UKUT 129 (LC). Where the factual basis of the alleged offence is disputed, those allegations must be tested by oral evidence and cross-examination; they cannot be determined solely on the papers: *Raza v Bradford Metropolitan District Council* [2021] UKUT 39 (LC).

The Tribunal's appellate jurisdiction is defined by paragraph 10 of Schedule 13A. An appeal is a rehearing (Sch.13A, para.10(3)). The Tribunal may confirm, vary or cancel the penalty (Sch.13A, para.10(4)) and may increase it up to the statutory maximum (Sch.13A, para.10(5)). It may have regard to matters of which the authority was unaware at the time of its decision (Sch.13A, para.10(3)(b)). The Final Notice is suspended pending determination of the appeal (Sch.13A, para.10(2)). The criminal standard of proof applies throughout. In *Waltham Forest LBC v Rahman* [2023] UKUT 139 (LC), the Upper Tribunal held that where new evidence revealed that the offence was more serious than originally appreciated, the Tribunal was entitled to increase the penalty accordingly.

A financial penalty may be imposed on both a company and its director where both are liable, but care must be taken to avoid effective double punishment. In *Sutton v Norwich City Council* [2021] EWCA Civ 20, the Court of Appeal confirmed that there is no statutory bar on imposing separate penalties on a company and its director, though the risk of overlap must be recognised. Likewise, joint owners may each receive penalties, with differences in culpability addressed through the level of penalty imposed: *Gill v Royal Borough of Greenwich* [2022] UKUT 26 (LC); [2022] H.L.R. 30.

If a financial penalty is not paid, the enforcement mechanism is contained in Schedule 13A. Where a person fails to pay the whole or any part of a financial penalty for which they are liable, the local housing authority may recover the penalty on the order of the county court as if it were payable under an order of that court (Sch. 13A, para. 11(2)). A certificate signed by the authority's chief finance officer stating that the amount due has not been received by a specified date is conclusive evidence of that fact in county court proceedings (Sch.

13A, para. 11(3)). A certificate purporting to be so signed is to be treated as valid unless the contrary is proved (Sch. 13A, para. 11(4)).

CHAPTER TWELVE

RENT REPAYMENT ORDERS

A rent repayment order ("RRO") is a statutory mechanism that enables rent paid to a landlord during a period of serious regulatory breach to be recovered. In practical terms, where a landlord commits certain housing offences, the tribunal may order repayment of rent received during the period of unlawful conduct.

The modern RRO framework in England applies to a wider category of housing offences but in the licensing context, the relevant offences are: Section 72 Housing Act 2004 control or management of a licensable HMO under Part 2 without a licence (see Chapters 2 and 3); and Section 95 Housing Act 2004 control or management of a house required to be licensed under Part 3 (selective licensing) without a licence (see Chapter 5).

These are strict liability offences (subject to statutory defences), discussed in detail in Chapter 10. Questions of who is the relevant "person having control" or "person managing" are addressed in Chapter 8. The procedural mechanics of licensing and appeals against licensing decisions are addressed in Chapter 7.

Where a person commits an offence under section 72 or section 95, the RRO regime permits recovery of rent received during the period of unlawful operation.

RROs were originally introduced by the Housing Act 2004 and applied in England and Wales. The Housing and Planning Act 2016

("HPA 2016"), in force from 6 April 2017, restructured the regime in England only.

The Renters' Rights Act 2025 ("RRA 2025"), which received Royal Assent on 27 October 2025, introduces further significant amendments to the English regime, including expansion of liability and extension of time limits. At the time of writing the Act is not yet in force but commencement of the principal RRO reforms is anticipated during 2026. Where relevant, those amendments are identified below.

In Wales provision is made for rent repayment orders by both the Housing Act 2004 and the Housing (Wales) Act 2014. The statutory position now differs materially between England and Wales and must be addressed separately.

Part A: England

RROs in England are governed by Chapter 4 of Part 2 of the Housing and Planning Act 2016.

Section 40(1) empowers the First-tier Tribunal (Property Chamber) to make a rent repayment order where a person has committed an offence to which the Chapter applies. Section 40(3) includes within the list of "*specified offences*" the licensing offences under section 72 and section 95 Housing Act 2004.

Section 40(2) limited liability to "*the landlord under a tenancy of housing in England*". In *Rakusen v Jepsen* [2023] UKSC 9; [2023] H.L.R. 21, the Supreme Court held that this wording confined liability to the immediate landlord only. It rejected the broader approach previously adopted in *Goldsborough v CA Property Management Ltd* [2019] UKUT 311 (LC); [2020] H.L.R. 18.

The RRA 2025 will amend section 40 so as to extend liability to superior landlords and to make clear that, where the offence is committed by a superior landlord, the provisions apply as if the housing were let by that superior landlord. Once in force, this amendment will reverse the practical limitation imposed by *Rakusen* and will be of particular importance in rent-to-rent and layered corporate structures.

The criminal standard of proof applies: Under section 43(1) HPA 2016, the tribunal must be satisfied beyond reasonable doubt that the offence was committed.

The RRA 2025 introduces provisions extending RRO liability to directors and similar officers of corporate landlords where the offence was committed with their consent, connivance or neglect. This aligns RRO liability more closely with the corporate liability framework discussed in Chapter 8.

In addition, the introduction of joint and several liability between landlords (where applicable) will be of practical importance where both immediate and superior landlords are implicated.

Quantum

Section 44 HPA 2016 governs the amount of an RRO in tenant applications. The tribunal must have regard to the conduct of the landlord; the conduct of the tenant; the landlord's financial circumstances; and whether the landlord has previously been convicted.

The Upper Tribunal in *Vadamalayan v Stewart* [2020] UKUT 183 (LC); [2020] H.L.R. 44 held that the starting point is ordinarily the statutory maximum, with deductions made for mitigation. The award is penal and deterrent rather than compensatory.

In *Williams v Parmar* [2021] UKUT 244 (LC); [2022] H.L.R. 7, the Tribunal emphasised that financial circumstances must be supported by evidence. In *Acheampong v Roman* [2022] UKUT 239 (LC), it reiterated the need for structured reasoning explaining how seriousness and mitigation have been assessed.

The RRA 2025 will amend section 44(4) to require the tribunal also to consider whether the landlord has previously received a financial penalty or been subject to an RRO. This reinforces the cumulative deterrent character of the regime.

Procedure (England)

Applications for a rent repayment order are made to the First-tier Tribunal (Property Chamber) under the Tribunal Procedure (First-tier Tribunal) (Property Chamber) Rules 2013.

An application may be brought by a tenant of the housing or by a local housing authority in respect of universal credit housing costs paid during the relevant period (section 41 HPA 2016).

Under the current regime, a tenant must apply within 12 months of the date on which the offence was committed or last committed. Once the amendments introduced by the Renters' Rights Act 2025 are commenced, that limitation period will extend to two years. Because offences under sections 72 and 95 Housing Act 2004 are continuing offences (*Luton BC v Altavon Luton Ltd* [2019] EWHC 2415 (Admin)) limitation will ordinarily run from the final day on which the property was operated without a licence.

Where the applicant is a local housing authority, it must first serve a notice of intended proceedings under section 42 HPA 2016. The notice must state that the authority intends to apply for an RRO, specify the reasons for the proposed application and the amount sought, and invite representations within a period of not less than 28 days. The landlord (or other proposed respondent) is entitled to make representations within that period. The authority must consider any representations received before deciding whether to proceed with the application. Failure to comply with these statutory requirements may render the application procedurally defective and susceptible to challenge.

Proceedings are commenced using the prescribed tribunal form, accompanied by a statement of case. Although tribunal pleadings are less formal than under the Civil Procedure Rules, the application must clearly identify the statutory offence relied upon (in licensing cases, usually section 72 or section 95 Housing Act 2004), the factual basis on which the respondent is said to be the relevant landlord, the period of unlawful operation, and the amount of rent paid during that period.

It is essential in licensing cases to establish that the property fell within a licensable category (see Chapters 2–5), that no licence was in force during the relevant period, and that the respondent was a "person having control" or "person managing" within section 263 Housing Act 2004 (see Chapter 8).

Although the proceedings are civil in form, the tribunal must be satisfied beyond reasonable doubt that the offence was committed (section 43(1) HPA 2016). The applicant therefore bears the burden of proving each element of the licensing offence. Evidence will typically include confirmation from the local authority as to licensing status, copies of tenancy agreements, proof of rent payments, and witness evidence addressing occupation and control.

Where the landlord relies on a statutory defence (for example, that a duly made licence application was pending or that there was a reasonable excuse) the tribunal must determine whether that defence is made out on the evidence (see Chapter 9).

The tribunal will usually issue case management directions requiring the respondent to file a response and for the parties to exchange witness statements and relevant documents. In straightforward cases where licensing status is uncontested, the matter may be determined on the papers. Where there is dispute as to control, management, designation, or reasonable excuse, an oral hearing will normally be listed and witnesses may be cross-examined.

If liability is established, the tribunal proceeds to determine quantum under section 44 HPA 2016 (see above).

Once made, an RRO is enforceable as a civil debt. If payment is not made voluntarily, the successful applicant must register the order in the county court and pursue enforcement through the usual mechanisms. Practitioners should consider enforceability at an early stage, particularly in rent-to-rent arrangements.

The tribunal's costs jurisdiction is limited. Costs may be awarded where a party has acted unreasonably in bringing, defending or conducting proceedings (rule 13), but there is no automatic costs shifting. This has practical implications for proportionality and litigation strategy.

Appeal lies to the Upper Tribunal with permission.

Local Authority Duties

Section 48 HPA 2016 provides that where a local housing authority becomes aware that a person has been convicted of a relevant offence, it must consider applying for an RRO in respect of that offence. Authorities must have regard to statutory guidance issued by the Secretary of State and must exercise their discretion consistently with public law principles and their published enforcement policies.

The RRA 2025 introduces a broader duty on local authorities to enforce landlord legislation in their area and strengthens investigatory and reporting frameworks. Although RROs are not expressly defined as "enforcement action" within every provision, they sit squarely within the reinforced enforcement landscape.

Part B: Wales

The rent repayment order regime in Wales differs materially from that in England. The scheme introduced by Chapter 4 of Part 2 of the Housing and Planning Act 2016 does not apply in Wales. Instead, rent repayment orders may arise under two distinct statutory frameworks:

Sections 73–74 of the Housing Act 2004 (licensing offences); and

Sections 32–33 of the Housing (Wales) Act 2014 (registration and activity-based licensing offences).

These regimes operate concurrently. The Housing (Wales) Act 2014 did not displace Parts 2 and 3 of the Housing Act 2004 in Wales; property-based HMO and selective licensing continue to apply. The 2014 Act introduced an additional, person-based licensing regime, with its own rent repayment provisions. It is therefore necessary to identify with care the statutory basis of any application.

Housing Act 2004

Sections 73 and 74 of the Housing Act 2004 provide for rent repayment orders in relation to certain licensing offences in Wales, namely: Section 72 (control or management of an HMO required to be licensed but not so licensed); and Section 95 (control or management of a house subject to selective licensing without a licence).

An application may be made to the Residential Property Tribunal (Wales) by a local housing authority or by an occupier of the premises (section 73(1)).

Where the application is made by a local housing authority, the tribunal must be satisfied beyond reasonable doubt that the landlord has committed the relevant offence (section 73(1), read with section 73(4)). A prior conviction is not required, but if there has been a conviction it is conclusive proof of the offence.

Where the application is made by an occupier, the tribunal may only make an order if the landlord has been convicted of the relevant offence (section 73(2)). In the absence of conviction, a tenant application cannot succeed. The criminal standard of proof therefore applies unless there has been a conviction.

If satisfied that the offence has been committed, the tribunal may make an order requiring the "appropriate person" to repay an amount not exceeding 12 months' rent (section 74(2)). The appropriate person is defined in section 73(10) as the person who at the time of payment was entitled to receive rent.

In determining the amount, the tribunal must have regard to the total rent paid during the relevant period and, in particular, any housing benefit or universal credit housing costs element paid in respect of the occupation (section 74(5)). The tribunal must also have regard to the conduct and financial circumstances of the landlord and, where relevant, the conduct of the occupier (section 74(6)). The statutory cap remains 12 months' rent.

Housing (Wales) Act 2014

The Housing (Wales) Act 2014 introduced a separate rent repayment order regime linked to offences under the person-based registration and licensing scheme. Section 32 provides that a rent repayment order may be made in respect of offences under: Section 7(5) (carrying out property management activities without a licence); and Section 13(3) (appointing or continuing to use an unlicensed agent where the landlord knows or ought to know of the absence of a licence).

Applications may be made by the licensing authority, by a local housing authority with the consent of the licensing authority, or by a tenant (section 32(1)).

Where the application is made by an authority, the tribunal must be satisfied that the relevant offence has been committed within the period of 12 months ending with the date of the application (section 32(4)). A prior conviction is not required in such cases. However, the authority must first serve a notice of intended proceedings explaining that it proposes to apply for an order, setting out the reasons, and inviting representations within a period of not less than 28 days (section 32(5)). The tribunal must be satisfied that such notice was served and that representations were considered before the application was made (section 32(6)).

Where the application is made by a tenant[1], the tribunal may only make an order if the landlord has been convicted of the relevant offence or has previously been the subject of a rent repayment order under section 32 in relation to the same dwelling (section 32(7)). The criminal standard of proof applies in the absence of conviction.

---

1 References to tenancy should be read as including occupation contracts under the Renting Homes (Wales) Act 2016.

Section 33 governs the amount payable. The maximum recoverable period is 12 months' rent (section 33(3)). The structure of the provision distinguishes between cases where there has been a conviction and housing benefit or the housing costs element of universal credit has been paid, and all other cases. Where the landlord has been convicted and housing benefit or universal credit housing costs have been paid in respect of the occupation, the tribunal must order repayment of the relevant amount, subject only to a power to reduce the amount if satisfied that there are exceptional circumstances (section 33(3)–(4)).

In other cases, the tribunal must consider the total amount of rent paid during the relevant period, the extent to which that rent was derived from benefit, any previous convictions of the landlord, and the conduct and financial circumstances of the landlord (section 33(6)). Where the application is made by a tenant, the tribunal must also consider the conduct of the tenant (section 33(6)(e)).

The structure of the 2014 Act regime therefore differs from that under the Housing Act 2004. In particular, tenant applications require a prior conviction or earlier order, and certain cases give rise to a mandatory repayment obligation subject only to exceptional circumstances.

CHAPTER THIRTEEN

BANNING ORDERS, MANAGEMENT ORDERS & THE ROGUE LANDLORD DATABASE

Where licensing breaches are serious or repeated, financial penalties and rent repayment orders may be insufficient. Parliament has therefore provided a further layer of regulatory control in Part 2 of the Housing and Planning Act 2016 ("HPA 2016"), enabling the exclusion of certain landlords and agents from the private rented sector altogether.

This chapter examines Banning orders (sections 14–26 HPA 2016) and The database of rogue landlords and property agents (sections 28–39 HPA 2016);

- Their interaction with licensing under the Housing Act 2004; and

- The procedural and evidential principles clarified by recent Upper Tribunal authority.

These provisions apply in England only.

Banning Orders

A banning order is an order made by the First-tier Tribunal (Property Chamber) prohibiting a person from: letting housing in England; engaging in letting agency work; engaging in property management work (section 14 HPA 2016).

Only a local housing authority may apply (section 15).

An application may be made only where the person "has been convicted" of a banning order offence (section 15(1)). The relevant offences are prescribed by the Banning Order Offences Regulations 2018 (SI 2018/216) and include, among others: offences under section 72 Housing Act 2004 (unlicensed HMO); offences under section 95 Housing Act 2004 (unlicensed selective licensing property); unlawful eviction offences; certain fraud and housing-related offences.

Before applying to the tribunal, the authority must serve a notice of intended proceedings (section 15). The notice must: be given within six months of the conviction (section 15(6)); specify the proposed banning order; state the length of the proposed ban; set out the reasons; allow at least 28 days for representations.

The proposed respondent is entitled to make representations within that period. The authority must consider any representations before deciding whether to apply. Compliance is mandatory. Failure to comply with section 15 may render the application procedurally defective.

The tribunal's jurisdiction arises under section 16 HPA 2016. It must consider: the seriousness of the offence; any previous banning order offences; whether the person is or has been entered in the rogue landlord database; the likely effect of the banning order on the person and others (section 16(4)).

In *Knapp v Bristol City Council* [2023] UKUT 118 (LC), the Upper Tribunal confirmed that the tribunal is not required to rehear the criminal case. It may give significant weight to the conviction and the sentence imposed when assessing seriousness (at [52]–[57]). The exercise is evaluative and discretionary.

The minimum duration of a banning order is 12 months (section 17(1)). There is no statutory maximum. The length must be proportionate to seriousness and risk.

Section 17(4) allows the tribunal to include exceptions, including transitional arrangements relating to existing tenancies. In *Knapp* (at [62]–[64]), the Upper Tribunal rejected the argument that banning orders apply only to future lettings. The prohibition may extend to the continued management of existing tenancies unless an exception is specified.

Appeal lies to the Upper Tribunal on a point of law. As confirmed in *Knapp* (at [38]–[39]), appellate intervention is limited to legal error.

The interaction between banning orders and the Rehabilitation of Offenders Act 1974 was clarified in *Hussain v Newham* LBC [2023] UKUT 287 (LC); [2024] H.L.R. 10. The Upper Tribunal held that the phrase "has been convicted" in sections 15 and 16 is not confined to unspent convictions (at [34]–[35]). A banning order may in principle be founded on a spent conviction. The tribunal is a "judicial authority" for the purposes of the 1974 Act and evidence of a spent conviction is admissible only if, under section 7(3) ROA 1974, justice cannot otherwise be done (at [45]).

Section 20 HPA 2016 permits variation or revocation where convictions become spent. This does not imply that only unspent convictions can found an order (*Hussain* at [34]).

A person subject to a banning order must not let housing in England; engage in letting agency work; engage in property management work (section 21). Breach is a criminal offence (section 21(3)), punishable by imprisonment or fine, or alternatively by civil penalty (section 23).

Schedule 2 HPA 2016 amended the Housing Act 2004 so that a person subject to a banning order cannot hold an HMO or selective licence. Existing licences may be revoked on fit and proper person grounds. Schedule 3 permits interim or final management orders to be made in respect of affected properties.

Section 27 contains anti-avoidance provisions preventing disposal of property to certain prohibited persons while subject to a banning order.

Management Orders

Where a landlord is prohibited from letting or managing housing, provision must be made to secure continued and lawful management of affected dwellings. Part 4 of the Housing Act 2004 provides for interim and final management orders.

Interim management orders ("IMOs") may be made under sections 102–104 Housing Act 2004 in prescribed circumstances. In the context of licensing enforcement, they most commonly arise where a licensable HMO or selective licensing property is unlicensed and there is no reasonable prospect of the property being licensed, or where a licence has been revoked and satisfactory alternative management arrangements are not in place. Schedule 3 to the Housing and Planning Act 2016 amended Part 4 to ensure compatibility with the banning order regime. Where a landlord becomes subject to a banning order and is thereby prohibited from managing property, the authority may consider making an interim management order to ensure that occupiers are protected and the property is properly managed.

An interim management order transfers to the local housing authority the right to possession (to the extent necessary to exercise management functions) and the right to collect rent. Ownership remains with the landlord, but management control passes to the authority. The authority is under statutory duties to manage the property effectively, having regard to the interests of occupiers and the landlord. An interim management order ordinarily lasts for a maximum of 12 months (section 104).

If, at the end of that period, the relevant statutory conditions continue to be satisfied, the authority may apply for a final management order under sections 113–116 Housing Act 2004. A final management order may last for up to five years. During its operation, the authority continues to exercise management functions and apply rental income in accordance with the statutory scheme, including payment of management expenses and other prescribed outgoings.

Management orders are therefore an integral part of escalated enforcement. A banning order excludes the landlord from participation in the sector; a management order provides the practical mechanism by which occupation and standards are maintained in the meantime. In serious licensing cases, the enforcement sequence may move from prosecution to banning order and, where necessary, to interim and then final management order.

Although management orders pre-date the banning order regime, they operate coherently with it. In practice, where a landlord is banned and no compliant alternative management arrangement is in place, consideration of a management order will frequently follow.

The Database of Rogue Landlords and Property Agents

Sections 28–39 HPA 2016 establish the database.

The Secretary of State must maintain the database (section 28). It is not publicly accessible but may be accessed by local housing authorities for enforcement purposes (section 39).

Where a banning order has been made following an authority's application, the authority must enter the person onto the database (section 29). Entry remains in force for the duration of the banning order.

Under section 30, an authority may enter a person where: the person has been convicted of a banning order offence; or the person has received two or more financial penalties within a 12-month period for such offences.

Before making an entry, the authority must serve a decision notice specifying the reasons and informing the person of their right of appeal (section 31). The person may appeal to the First-tier Tribunal (section 32). Entry must not occur until the appeal period has expired or any appeal has been determined.

Entry on the database is directly relevant to the fit and proper person assessment under sections 66 and 89 of the Housing Act 2004 and may materially affect future licensing decisions.

CHAPTER FOURTEEN

INVESTIGATORY POWERS

Part 7 of the Housing Act 2004 confers powers to require documents, to enter and inspect premises, to seek warrants, and to use information obtained under other statutory regimes. They also criminalise non-compliance, obstruction and the provision of false or misleading information.

These provisions apply in both England and Wales. The Renters' Rights Act 2025 amended aspects of the information and entry regime in England. Amendments to sections 235, 237 and 239 were brought into force on 27 December 2025. Unless otherwise stated, the underlying Housing Act 2004 framework remains intact.

Section 235 provides the principal documentary investigatory power. A person authorised in writing by a local housing authority may require the production of documents reasonably required for any purpose connected with the exercise of functions under Parts 1 to 4, or for investigating whether an offence has been committed under those Parts.

The documents must be "*reasonably required*" and the notice must specify or describe the documents sought, the time and place for production, and the person to whom they are to be produced. The notice must also inform the recipient of the possible consequences of non-compliance (section 235(3)).

The class of "*relevant persons*" upon whom a notice may be served is extensive. It includes licence holders or proposed licence holders under Parts 2 or 3, persons having an estate or interest, persons managing or having control (within the meaning of section 263), persons otherwise involved in management, and occupier. In practice, this enables authorities to obtain tenancy agreements, rent schedules, gas and electrical certification, management contracts, corporate ownership documentation, and communications relevant to control and management.

The statutory definition of "*document*" expressly extends to information recorded otherwise than in legible form; electronic records therefore fall squarely within the provision (section 235(6)).

Section 235 is subject to legal professional privilege. A person cannot be compelled to produce any document which he would be entitled to refuse to provide in High Court proceedings on grounds of privilege (section 235(5)).

Non-compliance is criminalised by section 236. A person who fails to do anything required by a section 235 notice commits an offence unless he has a reasonable excuse (section 236(1)–(2)).

Once the defence of reasonable excuse is raised, the prosecution must disprove it to the criminal standard. Section 236 further creates a distinct and more serious offence where a person intentionally alters, suppresses or destroys a document required to be produced (section 236(4)–(5)).

The deliberate destruction of rent records or occupancy documentation during a licensing investigation may therefore attract criminal liability independent of the underlying licensing breach.

Section 237 addresses the use of information obtained under other statutory functions, principally housing benefit and council tax powers. It permits a local housing authority to use such information for purposes connected with the exercise of functions under Parts 1–4 or for investigating offences under those Parts.

The Renters' Rights Act 2025 expanded the list of statutory purposes for which information may be used in England, extending it to enforcement under specified provisions of the Housing and Planning Act 2016 and the 2025 Act itself. The amendment, brought into force on 27 December 2025, does not create new powers of collection but clarifies and widens lawful cross-use of information already obtained. In Wales, section 237 continues in its pre-amendment form.

Section 238 creates offences relating to false or misleading information. A person commits an offence if he supplies materially false or misleading information to a local housing authority in connection with its Part 1–4 functions, knowing it to be false or being reckless as to its falsity (section 238(1)). A parallel offence arises where false information is supplied to another person with knowledge that it will be passed to the authority (section 238(2)).

The powers of entry are contained in section 239. An authorised officer may enter premises at any reasonable time where the authority considers that a survey or examination is necessary in order to determine whether functions under Parts 1–4 should be exercised, or where premises are subject to improvement notices, prohibition orders or management orders (section 239(1)–(3) . Entry ordinarily requires at least 24 hours' notice to the owner (if known) and to the occupier (section 239(5)). An exception exists where entry is required to ascertain whether an offence under section 72 (unlicensed HMO), section 95 (unlicensed selective licensing property), or section 234(3) (breach of HMO management regulations) has been committed. In such cases, entry may be effected without prior notice (section 239(6)–(7)).

Section 239 confers ancillary powers to take measurements, photographs and recordings, to bring equipment and assistants, and to take samples (section 239(8)). Authorisation must be in writing and must state the particular purpose for which entry is authorised (section

239(9)) and must be produced for inspection if requested (section 239(10)). Where premises are vacant or the occupier temporarily absent, the officer must leave them secured against trespassers (section 239(11)).

Where entry is refused, likely to be refused, or would be frustrated by notice, section 240 permits application to a justice of the peace for a warrant. The justice must be satisfied, on sworn information in writing, that admission is reasonably required and that one of the statutory preconditions is met, including refusal, temporary absence, or risk of defeating the purpose (section 240(4)). A warrant authorises entry by force if necessary (section 240(5)) and remains in force until its purpose is satisfied (section 240(9)).

Section 241 criminalises obstruction of an authorised officer exercising functions under Parts 1–4 or under sections 239 or 240. A defence of reasonable excuse is available.

Finally, section 243 governs the formalities of authorisation. Any authorisation for the purposes of section 235 or 239 must be given by the "appropriate officer" of the authority. Failure to comply with the statutory authorisation structure may render entry unlawful. Given that evidence gathered under sections 235–240 may underpin prosecution, civil penalties, rent repayment orders or banning order applications, strict compliance with authorisation requirements is essential.

PART IV

HOUSING LICENSING IN PRACTICE

CHAPTER FIFTEEN

PRACTICAL COMPLIANCE AND ENFORCEMENT STRATEGY

Housing licensing enforcement is adversarial by nature. For the local authority lawyer, the priority is robust decision-making that withstands tribunal scrutiny and protects the integrity of the licensing scheme. For the landlord's adviser, the focus is identifying procedural flaws, establishing statutory defences, and mitigating financial exposure. However, both sides operate within the same strict statutory framework where the margin for error is narrow. A missed deadline, a failure to secure evidence of "control," or a misunderstanding of the interaction between different enforcement regimes can be fatal to the case, whether one is prosecuting or defending.

Limitation and Deadlines

Unlike civil litigation, where extensions may often be agreed between parties, the timelines in the Housing Act 2004 are frequently absolute. Both parties must therefore monitor two distinct "hard" deadlines: the six-month limitation period and the 28-day appeal window.

For local authorities, the primary procedural risk lies in the six-month rule regarding the commencement of proceedings. Whether laying an information for a prosecution or serving a Notice of Intent to impose a civil penalty, the authority is bound by strict statutory time limits. In the case of civil penalties, Schedule 13A requires a Notice of Intent to be given before the end of the period of six months beginning with the first day on which the authority had "sufficient evidence" of the conduct. Where the offence is continuing, the notice may be served while the conduct continues or within six months of the last day of the conduct.

In practice, this makes the "date of knowledge" a critical battleground. Respondents will actively seek disclosure of when the authority's evidence was gathered to argue that a notice is out of time. Consequently, investigating officers must log the date on which sufficient evidence was obtained with precision, while defence practitioners must rigorously interrogate the timeline of the investigation.

For the respondent, the 28-day clock is equally unforgiving. Appeals against licence refusals, revocations, HMO declarations, and Final Notices for civil penalties must be made within 28 days. Similarly, written representations against a Notice of Intent must be submitted within the statutory 28-day window. This deadline triggers immediately upon service. For the authority, receiving late representations presents a strategic decision: waive the defect to ensure a robust decision that considers all matters, or stand on strict statutory rights? For the respondent, missing this window usually extinguishes the ability to challenge the underlying liability or quantum effectively.

Proving and Rebutting Liability

Successful enforcement and successful defence both rely on the same evidential tripod: establishing control, determining status, and assessing reasonable excuse.

The first challenge is establishing the "person having control" or "person managing." It is insufficient for an authority simply to identify the owner via the Land Registry. Liability under section 72 or section 95 depends on proving the receipt of rack-rent or the receipt of rent from occupiers under section 263. This is a strict factual test, not a title-based one. Authorities must therefore utilise their investigatory powers under section 235 to obtain tenancy agreements and bank statements to prove the flow of money. Conversely, practitioners acting for landlords must verify if their client actually fits the statutory definition. In complex structures involving "rent-to-rent" or lease-management agreements, the freeholder may well not be the "person managing" for statutory purposes, as discussed in Chapter 8.

The second area of contention is the defence of "reasonable excuse." This is the primary shield against criminal liability and civil penalties. For the respondent, evidence must be gathered immediately upon instruction. This includes logs of attempted applications, screenshots of failed online portals, and correspondence with managing agents. A vague assertion of ignorance is rarely sufficient. For the investigating officer, a robust investigation involves anticipating this defence. The "audit trail" of the landlord's interaction with the department should be reviewed before proceedings are issued to determine if the authority provided misleading advice or if the landlord made genuine attempts to comply.

Finally, where liability is admitted or proven, the focus shifts to quantum. For the authority, the penalty must adhere to their published enforcement policy. Deviating from the matrix without recorded reasons invites a tribunal to quash the decision on appeal. For the respondent, financial hardship must be evidenced, not merely asserted. The tribunal cannot reduce a penalty based on "ability to pay" without full financial disclosure, including accounts and tax returns.

Strategic Interplay

Practitioners on both sides must look beyond the immediate case to the wider consequences of the chosen enforcement route. Solving one legal problem may inadvertently trigger another.

The choice between Civil Penalty and Prosecution is the most significant strategic variable. For an authority, a Civil Penalty keeps the revenue within the local authority to fund housing enforcement, whereas a court fine is paid to the Treasury. However, a Civil Penalty does not result in a criminal conviction. Since a Banning Order requires a conviction, an authority seeking to ban a rogue landlord must pursue a prosecution, even if it is less financially advantageous to the council.

For the respondent, accepting a Civil Penalty avoids a criminal record. However, practitioners must advise clients that section 249A(5) only bars a subsequent prosecution for the same offence. It does not prevent a Rent Repayment Order or entry onto the Rogue Landlord Database. Crucially, an uncontested Civil Penalty is effectively an admission of the offence, which makes the defence of a subsequent Rent Repayment Order application extremely difficult.

Transitional Arrangements: The Renters' Rights Act 2025

As England moves into the regime established by the Renters' Rights Act 2025, all practitioners must remain alert to commencement dates and transitional provisions. The Act alters the enforcement landscape in two specific ways that affect current strategy.

First, regarding Rent Repayment Orders, the Act extends liability to superior landlords, reversing the Supreme Court's decision in *Rakusen v Jepsen*. For local authorities, this opens new targets for enforcement in "rent-to-rent" chains where the immediate landlord has no assets.

For respondents, it means superior landlords can no longer insulate themselves from the regulatory failures of their immediate inferior tenants; due diligence on intermediate leases becomes a critical compliance activity.

Second, regarding investigatory powers, the amendments to sections 235, 237, and 239 of the Housing Act 2004 allow for broader data sharing between departments for enforcement purposes. Practitioners must assume that information held by Council Tax or Housing Benefit departments is accessible to Licensing teams.

Conclusion

Housing licensing is a high-stakes regulatory environment. For the authority, the goal is effective regulation that improves housing standards. For the practitioner, the goal is protecting the client's position against significant financial and reputational liability. Success for either side requires the same approach: proactive case management, a forensic focus on the statutory definitions in the Housing Act 2004, and a clear understanding of the limitation clocks ticking in the background.

MORE BOOKS BY LAW BRIEF PUBLISHING

A selection of our other titles available now:-

'A Practical Guide to Probation Breaches and Other Applications' by Mark Thomas
'A Practical Guide to Remarriage and Divorce' by Cordelia Williams & Claire Howard
'A Practical Guide to Privacy, Transparency, Reporting Restrictions and Closed Proceedings in the Court of Protection' by Laura Mannering
'Beaumont on Barristers – A Guide to Defending Disciplinary Proceedings (Second Edition)' by Marc Beaumont
'A Practical Guide to Payments for Environmental Services' by Ben Sharples
'A Practical Guide to the Law of Pregnancy and Maternity at Work' by Rebecca Thomas
'A Practical Guide to Redundancy – Second Edition' by Philip Hyland & Collette Moore
'A Practical Guide to International Issues for Scottish Family Lawyers' by Susie Mountain, Donna McKay, Ken MacDonald
'A Practical Guide to the Law on Deprivation of Liberty' by Ben Troke
'A Practical Guide to Rights over Airspace and Subsoil – Second Edition' by Daniel Gatty
'A Practical Guide to the Law in Relation to Inquests' by Ramya Nagesh
'A Practical Guide to the Construction and Rectification of Wills and Trust Instruments (Second Edition)' by Edward Hewitt
'A Practical Guide to Data Protection in Social Housing' by Clare Paterson
'A Practical Guide to Spousal Maintenance – Second Edition' by Liz Cowell
'A Practical Guide to International Parental Child Abduction Law (England and Wales)' by Dr Onyója Momoh
'A Practical Guide to Deprivation of British Citizenship' by Sean Ell
'A Practical Guide to Commercial Property Service Charges' by Rachel Garton
'A Practical Guide to Clinical Negligence – Third Edition' by Geoffrey Simpson-Scott (Geoff)
'A Practical Guide to the Rights of Grandparents in Children Proceedings – Second Edition' by Stuart Barlow

'The Electronic Communications Code: A Practical Guide – Second Edition' by Kerry Bretherton KC, James Castle, Mark Loveday
'A Practical Guide to the Independent School Standards – September 2023 Edition' by Sarah McKimm
'A Practical Guide to Estate Administration and Crypto Assets' by Richard Marshall
'A Practical Guide to Parental Alienation in Private and Public Law Children Cases' by Sam King QC & Frankie Shama
'Contested Heritage – Removing Art from Land and Historic Buildings' by Richard Harwood QC, Catherine Dobson, David Sawtell
'The Limits of Separate Legal Personality: When Those Running a Company Can Be Held Personally Liable for Losses Caused to Third Parties Outside of the Company' by Dr Mike Wilkinson
'A Practical Guide to Transgender Law' by Robin Moira White & Nicola Newbegin
'A Practical Guide to 'Stranded Spouses' in Family Law' by Mani Singh Basi
'A Practical Guide to Residential Freehold Conveyancing' by Lorraine Richardson
'A Practical Guide to Pensions on Divorce for Lawyers' by Bryan Scant
'A Practical Guide to Challenging Sham Marriage Allegations in Immigration Law' by Priya Solanki
'A Practical Guide to Digital Communications Evidence in Criminal Law' by Sam Willis
'A Practical Guide to Legal Rights in Scotland' by Sarah-Jane Macdonald
'A Practical Guide to New Build Conveyancing' by Paul Sams & Rebecca East
'A Practical Guide to Inherited Wealth on Divorce' by Hayley Trim
'A Practical Guide to Practice Direction 12J and Domestic Abuse in Private Law Children Proceedings' by Rebecca Cross & Malvika Jaganmohan
'A Practical Guide to Confiscation and Restraint' by Narita Bahra QC, John Carl Townsend, David Winch
'A Practical Guide to the Law of Forests in Scotland' by Philip Buchan
'A Practical Guide to Health and Medical Cases in Immigration Law' by Rebecca Chapman & Miranda Butler
'A Practical Guide to Bad Character Evidence for Criminal Practitioners by Aparna Rao
'A Practical Guide to Extradition Law post-Brexit' by Myles Grandison et al
'A Practical Guide to Hoarding and Mental Health for Housing Lawyers' by Rachel Coyle

'Stephens on Contractual Indemnities' by Richard Stephens

'A Practical Guide to the EU Succession Regulation' by Richard Frimston

'A Practical Guide to Solicitor and Client Costs – Second Edition' by Robin Dunne

'Constructive Dismissal – Practice Pointers and Principles' by Benjimin Burgher

'A Practical Guide to Religion and Belief Discrimination Claims in the Workplace' by Kashif Ali

'A Practical Guide to the Law of Medical Treatment Decisions' by Ben Troke

'Fundamental Dishonesty and QOCS in Personal Injury Proceedings: Law and Practice' by Jake Rowley

'A Practical Guide to the Law in Relation to School Exclusions' by Charlotte Hadfield & Alice de Coverley

'A Practical Guide to Divorce for the Silver Separators' by Karin Walker

'The Right to be Forgotten – The Law and Practical Issues' by Melissa Stock

'A Practical Guide to Planning Law and Rights of Way in National Parks, the Broads and AONBs' by James Maurici QC, James Neill et al

'A Practical Guide to Election Law' by Tom Tabori

'A Practical Guide to the Law in Relation to Surrogacy' by Andrew Powell

'A Practical Guide to Claims Arising from Fatal Accidents – Second Edition' by James Patience

'A Practical Guide to Asbestos Claims' by Jonathan Owen & Gareth McAloon

'A Practical Guide to Stamp Duty Land Tax in England and Northern Ireland' by Suzanne O'Hara

'A Practical Guide to the Law of Farming Partnerships' by Philip Whitcomb

'A Practical Guide to the Law of Unlawful Eviction and Harassment – Second Edition' by Stephanie Lovegrove

'A Practical Guide to Costs in Personal Injury Claims – Second Edition' by Matthew Hoe

'A Practical Guide to the General Data Protection Regulation (GDPR) – Second Edition' by Keith Markham

'A Practical Guide to Working with Litigants in Person and McKenzie Friends in Family Cases' by Stuart Barlow

'Protecting Unregistered Brands: A Practical Guide to the Law of Passing Off' by Lorna Brazell

'A Practical Guide to Secondary Liability and Joint Enterprise Post-Jogee' by Joanne Cecil & James Mehigan

'A Practical Guide to the Pre-Action RTA Claims Protocol for Personal Injury Lawyers' by Antonia Ford
'A Practical Guide to Neighbour Disputes and the Law' by Alexander Walsh
'A Practical Guide to Coercive Control for Legal Practitioners and Victims' by Rachel Horman
'A Practical Guide to the Law of Driverless Cars – Second Edition'
by Alex Glassbrook, Emma Northey & Scarlett Milligan
'A Practical Guide to TOLATA Claims' by Greg Williams
'A Practical Guide to Elderly Law – Second Edition' by Justin Patten
'A Practical Guide to Responding to Housing Disrepair and Unfitness Claims' by Iain Wightwick
'A Practical Guide to the Law of Bullying and Harassment in the Workplace' by Philip Hyland
'How to Be a Freelance Solicitor: A Practical Guide to the SRA-Regulated Freelance Solicitor Model' by Paul Bennett
'A Practical Guide to Prison Injury Claims' by Malcolm Johnson
'A Practical Guide to Advising Clients at the Police Station' by Colin Stephen McKeown-Beaumont
'A Practical Guide to Antisocial Behaviour Injunctions – Second Edition' by Iain Wightwick
'Practical Mediation: A Guide for Mediators, Advocates, Advisers, Lawyers, and Students in Civil, Commercial, Business, Property, Workplace, and Employment Cases' by Jonathan Dingle with John Sephton
'The Mini-Pupillage Workbook' by David Boyle
'A Practical Guide to Crofting Law' by Brian Inkster
'A Practical Guide to the Law of Domain Names and Cybersquatting' by Andrew Clemson
'A Practical Guide to the Law of Gender Pay Gap Reporting' by Harini Iyengar
'NHS Whistleblowing and the Law' by Joseph England
'Employment Law and the Gig Economy' by Nigel Mackay & Annie Powell
'A Practical Guide to Noise Induced Hearing Loss (NIHL) Claims' by Andrew Mckie, Ian Skeate, Gareth McAloon
'An Introduction to Beauty Negligence Claims – A Practical Guide for the Personal Injury Practitioner' by Greg Almond
'Intercompany Agreements for Transfer Pricing Compliance' by Paul Sutton
'Zen and the Art of Mediation' by Martin Plowman
'A Practical Guide to Adoption for Family Lawyers' by Graham Pegg

'A Practical Guide to Industrial Disease Claims' by Andrew Mckie & Ian Skeate
'A Practical Guide to Conducting a Sheriff Court Proof' by Andrew Stevenson
'A Practical Guide to Vicarious Liability' by Mariel Irvine
'A Practical Guide to Applications for Landlord's Consent and Variation of Leases' by Mark Shelton
'A Practical Guide to Relief from Sanctions Post-Mitchell and Denton' by Peter Causton
'A Practical Guide to Equity Release for Advisors' by Paul Sams
'A Practical Guide to Financial Services Claims' by Chris Hegarty
'A Practical Guide to Financial Ombudsman Service Claims' by Adam Temple & Robert Scrivenor
'A Practical Guide to Running Housing Disrepair and Cavity Wall Claims – Second Edition' by Andrew Mckie & Ian Skeate
'A Practical Guide to Holiday Sickness Claims – Second Edition' by Andrew Mckie & Ian Skeate
'Arguments and Tactics for Personal Injury and Clinical Negligence Claims' by Dorian Williams
'A Practical Guide to Drone Law' by Rufus Ballaster, Andrew Firman, Eleanor Clot
'On Experts: CPR35 for Lawyers and Experts' by David Boyle
'An Introduction to Personal Injury Law' by David Boyle

These books and more are available to order online direct from the publisher at www.lawbriefpublishing.com, where you can also read free sample chapters. For any queries, call us on 0844 587 2383 or email us at mail@lawbriefpublishing.com.

Our books are all generally in stock at www.amazon.co.uk with free next day delivery for Prime members, and at good legal bookshops such as Wildy & Sons.

We are regularly launching new books in our series of practical day-to-day practitioners' guides. Visit our website and join our free newsletter to be kept informed and to receive special offers, free chapters, etc.

You can also follow us on Twitter at www.twitter.com/lawbriefpub.

www.ingramcontent.com/pod-product-compliance
Lightning Source LLC
LaVergne TN
LVHW022107200926
848481LV00003B/1087